Pioneering the Third Age

The Church in an Ageing Population

Pioneering the Third Age

The Church in an Ageing Population

Rob Merchant

First published in 2003 by Paternoster Press

09 08 07 06 05 04 03 7 6 5 4 3 2 1

Paternoster Press is an imprint of Authentic Media,
P.O. Box 300, Carlisle, Cumbria, CA3 0QS, UK
and
P.O. Box 1047, Waynesboro, GA 30830-2047, USA

Website: www.paternoster-publishing.com

British Library Cataloguing in Publication Data
A catalogue record for this book is available from
the British Library

ISBN 1-84227-177-6

Cover Design by FourNineZero
Typeset by WestKey Ltd, Falmouth, Cornwall
Printed in Great Britain by Cox & Wyman, Reading

'Rob Merchant's book is timely and trenchant. He brings to it a rare mix of gerontological knowledge, theological insight, pastoral sensitivity – and youth! He most helpfully points to a generational break between those becoming adult before and after about 1960. Churches, which have made varying efforts to communicate with young people in culturally appropriate ways, have totally failed to do the same regarding current and forthcoming cohorts of older people. Crucially, the latter tend to seek individual life fulfilment now not later – because death is regarded as the end to be postponed as long as humanly possible. However, cultural relevance is not the same as cultural conformity and he clearly shows how the Christian gospel honestly presented is in many ways counter-cultural. This book is affirming of older people and should stimulate evangelical and other churches to address the spiritual needs of those who have for too long either been taken for granted or devalued. This is a book to cherish – and act upon.'

Rev Albert Jewell, Former Pastoral Director and Senior Chaplain of Methodist Homes for the Aged

'Rob Merchant has addressed an area of church life and ministry which has been sadly overlooked, and has done so with enthusiasm, insight and commitment. This will be an essential resource for ministry in this field.'

Professor Alister McGrath, Principal of Wycliffe Hall, Oxford

'Here is some timely, accessible and revolutionary thinking about one of the urgent national issues of our day. For the first time in our history, the over-65s outnumber the under-16s. For many that is a ticking social time bomb, a disaster in the making. For Rob Merchant it opens up a riveting version for the church. I would have predicted that a combination of well-researched sociology, theology and senility would spell death to any publication! This book explodes that belief. It makes gripping reading for any Christian who wants to be a pioneer in the twenty-first century, and is an invaluable resource for today's church.'

The Rev Canon David MacInnes, Former Rector of St Aldates, Oxford

'This book is challenging to any stereotypical thinking about age, inspiring on the value of older people in our communities and fellowships and gives deep insights into the implications of current thinking. It is an enjoyable worthwhile stimulating read.'

Lady Gill Brentford, Third Church Estate Commissioner

'We are breaking new ground as older people – a recent remark by an older person to a gathering of local clergy led Rob Merchant to write this brief but very readable book. He sets out some of the principal insights and challenges about ageing today as found in current gerontological thinking, church pastoralia and social policy. He does not duck such emotive issues as ageism, pension rights and pensioner poverty. He gives all this thinking an appropriate scriptural context, and also shows how well read he is in the theories of the Early Church Fathers. His chapter on Basil of Caesarea and John Chrysytom is particularly illuminating.'

The Rev Canon Michael Butler, Vice-Chair of the Christian Council on Ageing

Contents

Foreword

For the first time in history the number of British pension-ers over sixty has exceeded the number of young people under sixteen. Within fifty years there will be in excess of two billion retired people in the world. This is bound to have profound implications for the economies of the world and particularly the West, where enhanced living condi-tions mean that most people live longer. Governments, hospitals, insurance schemes and employers are now being forced to take account of this rise of 'grey power'.

The churches might have been expected to give a lead in imaginative caring for pensioners, but unfortunately this is not the case. To be sure, the 'Third Age', the newly retired and still active, is more strongly represented in church circles than any other, but most churches do little to facilitate and empower older people as they draw near to the end of their life's journey. Rob Merchant is rightly criti-cal of this failure. He draws attention, in this ground-breaking book, to the urgent and increasing need for such ministry. He paints a fascinating and little-known picture of the church in the fourth century which he has carefully researched. They made care for the aged a sacred priority, and they present us with both a rebuke and an example. He points to ways in which the sheer life experience of older people can be an invaluable complement and corrective to contemporary youth culture, and can provide balance within the 'household of God'. Following St Chrysostom he prefers to think of 'full age' rather than 'old age', and offers this as a distinctively Christian contribution to gerontology. The believer is called to live life to a full age, however long it be, in terms of years spent in Christ's companionship, moulded and enriched by him, and leading not to extinction but to the day when we will know him fully.

This book is a wake-up call to the church, a subject for Christians to explore and pioneer, conscious of its urgency. The pioneers of the Wild West had a choice. But the pioneers of making a creative and fulfilling use of old age have no choice. It is a journey we must all take. And in the latter part of the book, the author gives shrewd insights into how it can be done.

Rob Merchant is an ideal person to write this book. In the first place he is a gerontologist who continues to research this area. Secondly, he is a practitioner who spends time with people in the Third Age, as he has with people with learning disabilities. Thirdly, he is a theologian who has wrestled with this issue for some years. And fourthly he is a minister of the gospel with a deep and compassionate concern as he calls on the churches to become pioneers of the Third Age. I commend this important book on a vital subject – and not just because I am well into the Third Age!

Michael Green, DD

Senior Research Fellow
Wycliffe Hall, Oxford University

Introduction

The world is changing before our eyes as ageing populations transform the landscape around us. Yet many do not
see this revolution in longevity. Its effects are being felt
economically, politically, technologically, in families, in
marriages, between generations, and in each of these areas
and more there is research being conducted by geront-
ologists across academic disciplines and the borders of
nations. Many have recognized the vast spiritual implications of these changes, the need to recover the value of
older age, seeking answers to spiritual quests, and tackling
the issues of older age and death. But few of these voices
are located within the church, and those that are find it
difficult to bring this revolution on to the agendas of
churches and leaders, whose attention is focused elsewhere. Though significant numbers of older people attend
a local church each week there is little training, little
teaching, and little understanding regarding the needs
in mission and discipleship for both current and future
generations of older people.

Pioneering the Third Age is offered as a starting point
from which to map out the territory of this new landscape
of older age that is being created. Its aim is not to provide
all the answers, because many of the questions have yet to
be asked about the older person and Christianity, but to

lift the attention of members and leaders of churches, regardless of age, to the landscape being changed around them and to begin to provide starting points from current gerontological thought, Scripture and the early church. The style is quick-fire and my intention is to surprise, provoke, and stimulate thought and debate.

A variety of sources have been combined in this text, from academic to popular, print to television, physical to electronic, and any mistakes that occur are my responsibility alone. I am deeply grateful for the encouragement of a number of people in this project. Michael Green who encouraged me to start writing and provided the opportunity to do so in *Church without Walls* (Paternoster Press, 2002). John Goddard of Paternoster Press, whose patient encouragement, stimulating ideas and willingness to support a newcomer to writing has been a tremendous and consistent blessing. To the staff and congregation of St John's I express my sincere thanks for the example they set in living for Jesus Christ as a family of believers. I am grateful to the Diocese of Birmingham for encouraging a newly ordained curate to take on a book project. To Professor Paul Kingston of Wolverhampton University, a patient PhD supervisor, and the staff of the Centre for Social Gerontology at Keele University I offer thanks for inspiring my interest in gerontology. My thanks also go to fellow members of the Evangelical Alliance's Reaching Older People Network for their welcome and friendship. And finally I must thank my wife, Tamsin, with whom I share life and ordained ministry, and without whose love, encouragement and patience this text would never have been completed.

Rob Merchant

Birmingham, UK, 2002

1

Our Present Situation

The situation is that my generation is a pioneering generation. My mother and father didn't live as long as I will, and
I've no one to show me how to grow old – we are breaking
new ground as older people. Who will show us the way?

An older woman shared this thought at a meeting for local
clergy I attended last year. It was a small local event, but
one that sparked my thinking.

The image of the 'pioneer' is tremendously helpful. It
conjures up something of the American West, the adventurers; the pioneers who set off on a trail of discovery,
urged on by the desire to discover new land, perhaps strike
it rich, always travelling into territory where no one of
their own society had gone before. While being a powerful
image, this analogy fails in one vital area: these pioneers
often had choices over the directions they were to travel in
and how they would actually travel. Our contemporary
pioneers of older age have not had the benefit of choosing
to live so long. Developments in standards of living and
medical technology mean that we live in societies able to
keep people alive longer than ever before.

These pioneers of older age are referred to as people
who are in their 'third' or 'fourth' age. These terms have
arisen as writers and researchers have sought to provide a

structure of age without reference to either 'the elderly' or 'the aged' – descriptions that throw together everyone above a certain age and are seen to represent the oppression of age. Referring to someone as being in his or her third or fourth age is considered more representative of the differing experiences of older people, regardless of actual age. The simplest description would be to describe someone in his or her third age as experiencing some form of retirement, having a good level of mobility, and managing his or her life without outside assistance. A person in his or her fourth age would be someone who requires physical assistance or care due to age-related disability, illness, or frailty caused by the process of ageing. This is not to suggest that those experiencing their fourth age are in some way less than those in their third age. The third and fourth ages contain the potential for the person to develop, to have expression, and to receive respect. Fears of the fourth age are often the result of older people themselves seeking to maintain the outward activity of their third age in our increasingly medicalized and consumption-driven societies.

The need to revise the language used when describing the experiences of older people has primarily been driven by the rapid increase in the numbers of people in their third and fourth ages. In 1901 about one-third of the population in the UK were under the age of 15, while just 5 per cent were over 65. In 1951 less than a quarter of the population were under 15, and more than 10 per cent were over 65.[1] Currently in the UK over 18 per cent of the population are over 65 (that's over 10.7 million older people) and this figure is only set to increase.[2] It is amazing that

---

[1] C. Phillipson, M. Bernard, M. Phillips and J. Ogg, *The Family and Community Life of Older People* (Routledge, 2001), p. 5.

[2] See the Age Concern Fact Sheet available online at < www.age concern.org.uk >.

over the last century the number of people over 65 has more than tripled, and over the last 50 years the figure has almost doubled.

These are changes of staggering proportions that will impact our society continuously over the coming decades. But such figures are not confined to the UK alone. The United Nations estimated in 1999 that the total world population over 60 years of age numbered 600 million people, with the largest percentage of older people living in Asia (53 per cent), and the next largest in Europe (25 per cent). However, it is predicted that in 2050 this 600 million will have grown to two billion people over 60 years of age. For the first time in human history the population of older people will be larger than that of children.[3] The pressure of such enormous changes in population structure will not be borne only by developed countries. Developing countries will face severe societal and economic strain, as their transition into ageing populations will take place in a compressed period of time, and without the social welfare provision available in many developed countries.[4] Reporting on the implications of an ageing world, the United Nations has observed:

> Demographers note that if current trends in ageing continue as predicted, a demographic revolution, wherein the proportions of the young and the old will undergo a historic cross-over, will be felt in just three generations. This portrait of change in the world's population parallels the magnitude of the industrial revolution – traditionally considered the most significant social and economic breakthrough in the

[3] 'Population Ageing 1999' published by the United Nations. Go to < www.un.org > and search for Population Ageing 1999 Press Release PI/1154 POP/734, 29 June 1999.
[4] Ibid.

history of humankind ... The demographic revolution, it is envisaged, will be at least as powerful.[5]

We are standing in the midst of a revolution that Kofi Annan, the Secretary General of the United Nations, has described as being economic, social, cultural, psychological and spiritual.[6] Tremendous societal changes are rushing past us: pioneers are journeying into whatever the future may hold; new cultural expressions are forming; old cultural norms are disintegrating. Yet where are the voices calling out with the distinctive voice of Jesus in the midst of this revolution? Who is answering the plea of our pioneer of the third age: 'we are breaking new ground as older people. Who will show us the way?'

One of the most important lessons learnt from mission work with younger people has been the need to understand the issues that those younger people face: their lifestyles, influences, role models, their aspirations and expectations. Each of these aspects remains true for older people. Time must be taken to map the territory through which our current generation of pioneers have already travelled.

I once heard an academic give an illustration of the way some older people find it hard to accept new technology (an unfortunate and sweeping generalization). The illustration he used was of his mother, who had always refused

---

[5]   < www.un.org/esa/socdev/ageing/ageimpl.htm > (accessed 19 May 2002).

[6]   K. Annan, 'A "Society for All Ages" honours traditional leadership role of elders, Secretary-General says, opening International Year of Older Persons' (a statement by the Secretary General of the United Nations, Kofi Annan, made at a ceremony launching the International Year of Older Persons in 1999). Go to < www.un.org/esa/socdev/iyop/iyopsgsm.htm > (accessed 14 May 2002).

to have a microwave because she didn't want a nuclear bomb in her kitchen! At first the speaker's incredulity at this understanding of a useful piece of kitchen equipment would appear reasonable. But if we take just a few moments to consider the world his mother experienced we might begin to see the culturally loaded understanding she carried with her.

This lady would have experienced the Second World War, ended by the dropping of atomic bombs on Hiroshima and Nagasaki, killing hundreds of thousands of people through both the blast effects and radiation poisoning. She would have seen the Iron Curtain falling across northern Europe, and the start of the cold war arms race, with the detonation and trials of evermore-powerful nuclear weapons. The 1960s witnessed the Cuban Missile Crisis, when the world came to the brink of nuclear war; newspapers, television and radio carrying news of the USSR's positioning of missiles that could penetrate the USA with only five minutes' warning. She would have seen cinema and television information films about what to do in the event of a nuclear attack, the risk of radiation, and the threats posed to her family. The link between nuclear bombs and radiation fallout was stark and the message clear. It is little wonder that when she discovered microwaves cooked using 'radiation' (regardless of its safety or form) she wouldn't allow one in her kitchen. She had spent her whole life at risk, and now she was being asked to bring something she understood as being the cause of that risk into the safety of her own home!

Admittedly, this is only one illustration from one person's life, and I know one 90–year-old man who happily uses a microwave. Some pioneers travel light, they have crossed territory and have left it behind, but many continue to carry with them learnt behaviour and past memories that affect present expectations. Reaching out with the good news of Jesus Christ and discipling older people means taking time to understand the territory they have navigated and traversed as generational pioneers. By understanding the journeys people have made and the different types of territory they have crossed it is possible to begin to grasp the issues faced now.

The rest of this chapter provides a whistle-stop tour of some of the issues that form the contemporary debate surrounding older age. They are not intended as definitive explanations, but to provide a starting point from which further examination can be pursued. Understanding the issues facing older people today is vital, not only for those pioneering this new territory, but for those engaging in mission to and discipleship of men and women in their third and fourth ages, and for all of us who will one day experience our own third and fourth ages.

Ageism

> Ageism allows the younger generation to see older people as different from themselves: thus they suddenly cease to identify with their elders as human beings and thereby reduce their own dread of ageing ...[7]

Over the last twenty years the term 'ageism' has increasingly found its way into contemporary language and has formed the starting point for the majority of gerontological research.[8] Ageism exists at all levels of our society. For example, some commentators argue that the existence of a

---

[7] R.N. Butler quoted in S. Biggs, *Understanding Ageing: Images, Attitudes and Professional Practice* (Open University Press, 1993), p. 85.

[8] Ibid. p. 86.

compulsory state retirement age in the UK is an example of ageism in structural form. Prejudices towards older people are also expressed in everyday language. Describing someone as an 'old biddy', an 'old duffer' or an 'old dear' may seem at first to be innocent; however, such terms are loaded with meaning, denying the older person is someone of importance in God's economy. Ageism can also be seen in the church today. Personally, I have lost count of the number of times I have heard leaders of churches complain that the problem with their church is the older members: '*They* are the ones who don't want to see change' is all too often the charge laid at the feet of older people. Albert Jewell recalls conducting a seminar for ministers and discovering that 'none of their churches had formulated mission statements or strategies that gave any priority to the needs of older people'.[9] An older person's experience of society is too often either taken for granted or considered irrelevant. When the same experiences spill over into the church it is hardly surprising that older members can mount a determined resistance to change, especially if they feel they have been excluded from the process of decision-making. Ageism is expressed at times in Christian literature: recent references like 'the oldies are coming back' in relation to church attendance surveys are unfortunate, indiscriminately lumping several generations of older people together, and so failing to recognize the value and distinctiveness of the older person.

It is the 'dread of ageing' that underpins ageism, affecting attitudes towards older age and therefore towards older people themselves. Many different types of people, including church leaders who are themselves ageing, can experience a fear of ageing. However, this fear of age and

---

[9] A. Jewell (ed.), *Older People and the Church* (Methodist Publishing House, 2001), p. 1.

the aged is hardly a recent phenomenon. The ancient philosopher Seneca gave what is considered to be one of the most heartfelt and emphatic observations of old age surviving from antiquity:

> I shall not abandon old age, if old age preserves me intact for myself, and intact as regards the better part of myself; but if old age begins to shatter my mind, and to pull its various faculties to pieces, if it leaves me, not life, but only the breath of life, I shall leap from a building that is crumbling and tottering.[10]

Satirists such as Juvenal in the second century AD identified old age with a wrinkled, sagging face, a shaky voice and limbs, a bald head and toothless gums.[11] When analysing views regarding old age from antiquity, as will be explored later in this book, there are many negative descriptions of old age and few that are positive.

The real difficulty with ageism is that it exists beneath the surface in our expectations and language and can so easily slip out when you least expect it. Quite simply, ageism can catch you by surprise. During my training for ordination I took part in a college-based mission that was led by the evangelist Michael Green. The mission proved an important time in identifying the ageist attitudes that lay within my own life. During one outreach event I watched Michael, a smiling and congenial older gentleman, stereotyping him without realizing it. In the space of ten minutes he had talked about Jesus with families, single people, bikers, children, and without anyone rejecting his approach! I had wrongly assumed that as an older person

[10] T. Parkin, 'Ageing in Antiquity: Status and Participation' in P. Johnson and P. Thane (eds), *Old Age from Antiquity to Postmodernity* (Routledge, 1998), p. 28.

[11] Ibid. p. 32.

he wouldn't be able to do that: surely people would think him just some nice old slightly eccentric Englishman and ignore him. My mind had put a limit on him, which then limited my expectations of what God could do through him, simply on the basis of his age. How utterly and completely wrong I was! Michael returned with the contact details of two people, had prayed with one, and had invited another family along to an evening event, to which they duly came. Praise God that it was the wisdom of age in charge that day and not the attitude of ageism!

There are commentators who view the church as a sponsor of ageist attitudes. Steve Scrutton observes:

> Ageism is firmly embedded in the values and beliefs of Christianity ... Religious attitudes can prevent older people from questioning their social status and situation, and stop them developing a level of dissatisfaction that might otherwise prove embarrassing to dominant ideologies.[12]

I do not agree that ageism is embedded in Christianity itself. However, the absence of developed and cohesive theological discussion around ageing is an example of the church failing to equip older people, and those who minister to them, with the knowledge and understanding to consider their status and situation from within Christianity.

Pensions: Poverty and Wealth

In March 2001 the total number of people in receipt of a retirement pension in the UK was 11 million. The number of men included in this figure was less than 4.1 million

---

[12] S. Scrutton, *Counselling Older People* (Arnold, 1999²), p. 14.

whereas the number of women was around 7 million. This difference is primarily because women live longer than men. However, statistics are never that simple, and recent evidence has shown how life expectancy can also be linked to social class. For a man in a professional social class, life expectancy is 78.5 years, while if the same man were in an unskilled social class, his life expectancy would drop to 71.1 years. Similarly, for a woman in a professional social class, life expectancy is 82.8 years, whereas if the same woman were in an unskilled social class, her life expectancy would drop to 77.1 years.[13] There remains a difference in life expectancy based upon whether you are male or female; but the more significant effect upon longevity is whether or not you are experiencing poverty. The issue of pensioner poverty is an ever-present concern for many older people. In 1998 the Rowntree Foundation reported that 30 per cent of pensioners were in the bottom fifth of total income distribution. The effects of poverty in an older person's life were identified as increased risk of ill health, disability, anxiety, and low spending on basic commodities such as food.[14]

The picture regarding pension provision is changing. In 1999–2000 73 per cent of pensioners had some form of investment income, whilst 59 per cent of pensioners received an income from an occupational pension.[15] An article in *The Guardian* newspaper in 1999 highlighted the

---

[13] *Trends in Life Expectancy by Social Class 1972–1999* (Office of National Statistics, 2002), p. 1.

[14] *Findings* (Joseph Rowntree Foundation, December 1998). *Findings* is a briefing paper format of a larger report, *Monitoring Poverty and Social Exclusion: Labour's Inheritance*, by Catherine Howarth, Peter Kenway, Guy Palmer and Cathy Street, published by the Joseph Rowntree Foundation, York, UK.

[15] *Pensioners' Incomes Series 1999/00* (Office of National Statistics, 2000), p. 8.

growing difference in wealth between the generations of older people. Utilizing the results of a survey, the article examined the 'two-thirds' world of old age, observing that couples under the age of 75 tended to own their own homes and had occupational pensions, while people over 80 years of age struggled to live on £80 a week or less in state benefit. 'While the majority [of respondents], 90%, enjoyed retirement', reported the article, 'a small but significant group faced a bleak old age.'[16] The most significant group of people who face that 'bleak old age' is older women, usually widows, who can face significant hardship and risk in older age. This danger increases further if the individual is not only a single older woman, but also from an ethnic background, which may have meant her living with the experience of poverty throughout her life – all of which is borne out by US research.[17]

We will explore further in the following chapter how the gap between poorer and wealthier older people is only set to increase over the coming years.

Retirement

We have reached the stage where retirement is accepted as a 'normal' experience; one should expect to leave active economic participation in a national workforce on the basis of age. However, retirement is a modern construct. Admittedly, there has always been a certain percentage of older people who have ceased to be active workforce

---

[16] S. Hall, 'Half Over 80s Exist on £80 a Week or Less', *The Guardian*, 5 October 1999.

[17] F. Lomax Cook and R.A. Settersten, 'Expenditure Patterns by Age and Income among Mature Adults: Does Age Matter?', *The Gerontologist* Vol. 35 No. 1 (The Gerontological Society of America, 1995), pp. 10–23.

participants, and historically this has been due to exclusion on the grounds of poor health. It has only been since the Second World War that we have seen a state retirement policy enacted, which has brought about what is described as the 'retirement tradition'.[18] For many older people who were pioneers in this developing tradition, retirement was seen as something that was to be held off, as it continued to be characterized as a time of crisis and sickness. However, in the recession-hit 1970s and 1980s, a time marked by mass unemployment, instead of being something to be actively feared retirement became a matter of active choice, and the practice of early retirement developed.[19] It is fascinating that in the UK we now see situations where this practice has become a public policy issue. For example, in the case of teachers, the government stopped the process of early retirement due to ever-increasing pension and recruitment/training costs. No longer forced upon many people due to ill health, retirement has become a matter of choice, and this choice is further evidenced by a developing consumer culture of retirement.

The existence of choice would seem to imply that retirement is only about opportunity, but it is also one of the most marked periods of change for any person in his or her life's course. It can bring stress to families, marriages, friendships and faith, yet we seem to expect older people to cope with their changing situation alone. As a minister I find it strange that we prepare people for marriage and for baptism, we support people in grief and rally round when a child is born, but retirement seems to pass us by. Perhaps it is that retirement is not a sacrament of the church, so it

---

[18] A. Blaikie, *Ageing and Popular Culture* (Cambridge University Press, 1999), p. 62.

[19] Ibid. p. 63.

doesn't fall into the church calendar. Also, the times at which people retire alter, as do their experiences of financial readiness. Alternatively, perhaps it is because Scripture doesn't contain any notion of 'retirement'.[20] Meeting Bishop Moses Tay at a prayer summit in Malaysia after his retirement from the elected post of Archbishop of South East Asia, he described himself not as 'retired' but as 're-tyred', renewed and ready to continue serving God. It is a wonderful image that we can continue to serve God into retirement. The difficulty is finding the help to be able to make that transition. The grief of losing one's role and sense of purpose can be acute; the change in relationship as either one or both marriage partners find themselves in the home can be particularly stressful. Australian research of the early 1990s indicated the difficulty of a change of relationship when the retiring husband entered into the previously 'husband-free zone' of the home, in which the wife had control of daily events. This changing situation had the potential to bring tremendous strain to the marriage relationship. The UK sitcom *Keeping up Appearances* gave a humorous portrayal of the implications of retirement: one episode showed Richard (the retiring husband) pleading with his employer not to make him retire and spend any more time at home with his wife, Hyacinth, than was necessary.

---

[20] The only biblical reference to retirement comes in Numbers 8:25 where those aged 50 are to end their active service in the Tent of Meeting but are permitted to continue to assist their brothers with duties, though not carrying these out themselves. While accepting that there is a process of withdrawal from the heavy work of the Tent of Meeting, there remained some form of participation, and no loss of Levitical status is implied. To describe this as some form of retirement as we currently understand it with its withdrawal, lack of participation, and loss of status would be to read back into Scripture a modern construct.

It will be fascinating to watch research and debate unfold as increasing numbers of men and women who have both been economically active throughout their lives suddenly find themselves thrown together in the post-retirement environment either by choice or financial necessity. There is little available research about changing divorce rates amongst older people at present; however, divorce could well become an increasing experience in older age, facilitated by greater financial independence for both partners.

Sexuality

The general assumption that older people fit some kind of heterosexual 'norm' hides a whole sub-culture of older people for whom gender issues are far from straightforward. Having lived through eras in which same-sex relationships were described as socially and criminally deviant, there is now increasing freedom of expression among mature gay people. The influence of expressive younger generations can be frequently seen as influencing those older generations in which expression was repressed. Whether one agrees or not with homosexual relationships, the proliferation of web sites, clubs and magazines aimed at the older, and often more affluent, gay man or woman is noticeable.

Preparing for a small presentation for the National Assembly of Evangelicals I came across a striking picture of two older men, Roy and William, both in their 70s, who had lived together for over 50 years. Perhaps the key to this image was not just, 'Yes, older people can be gay too', but rather that the world in which we live is rapidly changing. We have witnessed the growing willingness of organizations representing people who are gay to utilize the media, campaigns and lobbying to present a very public image of young gay people. This acceptance will carry over into the relationships of older gay people as they realize that their relationships are no longer to be hidden from society.

Contrary to popular opinion older people are sexual beings and sexual interest and activity are continued throughout life.[21] This realization has been recently reinforced by the media attention focused on new forms of medication such as Viagra and Estratest, which have enabled many older people to give renewed expression to their sexuality. Anecdotal evidence from news articles appears to support this growing expression: one journalist has commented, 'I recently met someone who returned from a Saga holiday to report that it was "hooching with sex", the clients having discovered the joys of a good time without the threat of pregnancy.'[22] But this newfound lease of sexual expression has also brought unforeseen consequences. American research has drawn attention to data demonstrating that 'AIDS risk in older adults is more common than previously believed, with unprotected sex a significant route of infection.'[23] A more moving account of this increasing risk comes from an older person who discovered she was HIV positive aged 55 in 1991. The article is published on the web site for the

---

[21] D. Jerrome, 'Intimate Relationships' in J. Bond, P. Coleman and S. Peace, *Ageing in Society* (Sage, 1993²), p. 246.

[22] C. Boyle, 'Love in an Older Climate', *The Guardian*, 20 July 2000.

[23] K.E. Radda, J.J. Schensul, G.J. Burkholder, E. Ward and J. Levy, 'Intimate Contacts: Older Adults at Risk, Sexual Activities and HIV Risk' in programme abstracts from the 54th Annual Meeting of the Gerontological Society of America, *The Gerontologist* Vol. 41 Special Issue 1, October 2001 (The Gerontological Society of America, 2001), p. 8.

Association of Retired Persons over 50 (AARP). Reflecting on the actor Rock Hudson's own death through Aids-related illness, she writes:

> Hudson was just shy of 60 when he died. He was my first indicator that AIDS was not just a young person disease ... 20 years ago, people aged 50 and older accounted for 11 percent of AIDS cases in the United States. Today, in some parts of the country, that number is 15 percent. Between 1991 and 1996, AIDS cases rose more than twice as fast among older persons than younger adults. The number of older men infected with HIV through heterosexual contact jumped by 96 percent, while heterosexual transmission among women 50 and older increased by 106 percent.[24]

New forms of medication to enable sexual function are not the primary cause of this increasing risk to the sexual health of older people. But they have enabled older people to express sexual desire more freely and readily than at any other point in history. The march of medical technology brings with it both opportunities and consequences. I wonder how many of our churches realize the need to teach Christian sexual morals and responsibility to people of all ages?

An earlier section alluded briefly to the financial inequalities that older women face. The issue of gender differences finds expression in many areas: we have already outlined those that could be considered ageist in a more general sense. However, older women face not only ageism, but also sexism. This distinction between men and women often finds expression through the stereotype

---

[24] J.P. Fowler, 'Why Me? The Truth about HIV' at < www.aarp. org/mmaturity/jul_aug00/whyme.html >. First published 2000.

that men can grow old gracefully whereas women are merely faced with a life of steady decline. Consider for a moment the images you see in advertising, on television, or in the movies. American research into the contents of jokes, cartoons and birthday cards concluded that negative images had a greater occurrence than positive: 'Longevity, physical and mental disability, un-attractiveness and sexual disability predominated, while jokes about elderly women were more negative than those about men.'[25] Although, as will be shown in Chapter 5, such negative stereotypes of the older woman have existed from antiquity, the challenge for the church is to recover the value that God sees in the older woman.

Healthcare

To mark the passing of the year 2000 the polling company Gallup conducted a millennium survey of 50,000 people across 60 countries in which it asked the question: 'What matters most in life?' The answer 'To have good health' was the number one reply in 37 out of the 60 countries and overall 'health' was one of the top two replies in 50 out of the 60 countries polled. Health is a vital issue for all ages and the issue of health in older age is without doubt one of the most significant for older people.

Evidence relating to healthcare provision in the UK reports that in 1998 59 per cent of people aged 65–74 and 66 per cent of people aged 75+ reported a long-standing illness. Long-term illness has tremendous implications for the person wanting to make the most of his or her third or fourth age. The organization Age Concern has

---

[25] Research by E.B. Palmore, quoted in Blaikie, *Ageing and Popular Culture*, p. 98.

observed that 38 per cent of people aged between 65 and 74 and 50 per cent of those aged 75+ have some form of long-standing illness that limits their lifestyle. Further, in 1998 it was estimated that approximately 5 per cent of the population aged 65+ and 20 per cent of the population aged 80+ suffered from dementia. In the space of one week in 1998 it was estimated that over 368,500 households with members aged 65+ received home help or home-care services.[26]

The challenge that the above statistics hold for the provision of care is simply its necessity. With 50 per cent of those currently aged 75+, approximately 2.15 million people, enduring some form of long-standing debilitating illness at some point, care is required in a society operating a welfare system that includes a national healthcare service. But for such services to exist and for care to be provided financial support is needed, and as an economics teacher would constantly remind me, 'There's no such thing as a free lunch!'

The societal burden faced is principally one of economics. Age Concern has stated that about 40 per cent of total hospital and community health service expenditure is on people aged 65+. The largest part of National Health Service spending in the UK is on hospital and community health services, discretionary family health services and related services: figures for 1999–2000 gave an estimated forecast of a £33,784 million net spend in this area.[27] Therefore, if we take Age Concern's figure of 40 per cent, the cost of caring for people aged 65+ in 1999–2000 was approximately £13.5 billion. This represents not only the cost of

---

[26] Age Concern Fact Sheet at < www.ageconcern.org.uk >.

[27] Government Expenditure Plans 2000–2001. These figures from the Department of Health can be viewed at < www.doh.gov.uk/dohreport/report2000/dr2000–03.html >, see Fig. 3.14.

care, but also the burden for the taxpayer, as 77 per cent of National Health Service funding comes from general taxation.[28] Difficulty comes with the realization that, while the older population is set to continue its expansion, the number of people of working age contributing into a national tax system will have decreased.

I am not complaining that too much is spent on caring for older people and my description of the provision of care as a 'burden' could, rightly, be considered emotive. However, my aim is simply to outline the ever-increasing expenditure required by an ageing population, which could lead to increased generational tension as younger generations provide the necessary taxation to fund a public health service that successive governments have failed to invest in long term. This financial cost has led some commentators to describe an ageing population as a demographic time bomb. In this understanding the collateral damage is primarily viewed in financial terms for younger generations. But this interpretation of the future is being increasingly challenged and my own view is that to provide such a system of care free at the point of delivery through general taxation is a good and right burden to be carried. People who have lived to old age by definition have lived through all the earlier stages of life in which they contributed to a common social good – as workers, parents, friends, neighbours, and in many cases contributors to a national war effort.[29] To express this in more simple and factual terms, when using healthcare services, the older person is only using that which he or she has spent a lifetime contributing to.[30]

---

[28] Ibid. Fig. 3.15.

[29] M. Johnson, 'Dependency and Interdependency' in Bond, Coleman and Peace, *Ageing in Society*, p. 262.

[30] J. Landale, L. Peek and G. Jacob, 'Blair Urged to Buy Back the Pensioner Vote', *The Times*, 15 May 2000.

Dementia

Health statistics suggest that with increasing age comes increasing risk of dementia. The form of dementia most commonly known is Alzheimer's disease. This is only one type of dementia, and is not only experienced by older people, but it is a condition predominantly found amongst older age groups. James Saunders has written an excellent Grove booklet on this subject, which is an insightful and helpful outline. He observes one description of dementia as 'a return to chaos', serving as a reminder of the confusion and disintegration that dementia can bring into the life of the individual.[31] Saunders continues, offering the following description:

> The experience is of a desperate search for order with which to hold off threatening chaos; of endless improvisation as one longs for stability and time; and of life in the 'eternal "now"' while seeking to fix a past and a future. Although drifting apart from the world, the dementia sufferer is trying desperately to maintain contact.[32]

One of the most remarkable illustrations I have come across of the effects of Alzheimer's was in an article by the daughter of American President Ronald Reagan. She likened watching the development of her father's illness to watching a beautiful pearl necklace fall on to a floor and break apart, only being able to look on as one by one each pearl rolled away to be lost forever. I was recently sharing this picture with a member of the congregation in which I serve when John, who had been listening, challenged the

---

[31] J. Saunders, *Dementia: Pastoral Theology and Pastoral Care* (Grove, 2002), p. 6.

[32] Ibid. pp. 6–7.

assumption of only ever seeing decline with Alzheimer's. John had nursed and supported his wife through Alzheimer's over a number of years and he observed that, while pearls were indeed lost, new pearls could be discovered. He recalled watching his wife when he collected her from a short period of respite care. Before leaving she went around the main room in the respite centre holding the hands of each of person there. She moved slowly around the room, careful to take time with each person. Wondering what she was doing, John suddenly realized that his wife was going round and praying with each individual. Though unable to speak and having lost a significant amount of ability through Alzheimer's, here was a new pearl that John watched being drawn out of the depths of his wife's life, brought into the brightness of the day.

Much is being done in both in theory and practice in the area of reaching the person with dementia with Christ's love and of sustaining the faith of Christians who have dementia. The often-used generalization of the way in which older people with dementia can seem to re-engage for a moment through the Lord's Prayer, or a familiar hymn, is true. But for how long these points of contact remain available is uncertain. Perhaps the tragedy of the future will be older generations of people who will not have had that same experience of religion still retained by today's generations; who will not have the same depth of religious experience to draw upon to sustain them as they seek to maintain contact with the world in which they live.

Death and Dying

Having briefly looked at issues of retirement, potential poverty, healthcare, the demand for health and the sufferings brought by dementia, it is little wonder that death and dying must be included. In a world in which the demands of the individual are increasingly about the quality of life to be lived now, coupled with a decline in religious belief, it is little wonder people fear not death but the process of death itself. We live in a society in which hope is increasingly absent from people's view of life and the issue of the individual's value is paramount. In an article on the subject of euthanasia, Danish researchers suggested that:

> Dignity and being independent of others have a high value in the quality of life of elderly people … Pain and death are not the most threatening situations older patients fear, it is continued degradation they do not accept.[33]

Euthanasia literally means 'a good death'. Tony Walter in his book *The Revival of Death* describes how supporters of euthanasia view a 'good death' as one that is under the dying person's control. Walter observes that:

> The obsession of doctors with maintaining life at all costs and the dogmas of religion about life being the gift of God rather than the possession of the individual, are rejected in favour of the authority of the dying self to determine its own end.[34]

It is fascinating how consumerism has spilled over into our understanding of life and its value. If we are able to continue to consume life, then let us live it; if we are unable to consume life and are facing illness that will slowly starve consumption, then let us die. However, viewing the debate surrounding euthanasia as consumerism run

---

[33] T. Scheper and S. Duursma, 'Euthanasia: The Dutch Experience' in *Age and Ageing* (Oxford University Press, 1994), p. 7.

[34] T. Walter, *The Revival of Death* (Routledge, 1997), pp. 29, 152–6.

wild alone is simplistic. Walter observes the tendency to define the person as utterly and totally separate from God or any sense of 'other'; as it is left to the 'dying self' to determine its own end. Zygmunt Bauman, a sociologist, has observed how people live 'credit card' rather than 'savings account' lives. When there is nothing in the savings account to carry you forward and the credit card has reached its limit there doesn't appear to be much choice left for the consuming self.

There are points at which the withdrawal of medical or life support, which only serve to sustain and not improve life, would appear to be appropriate. But the active choice of the individual to end his or her life in order to die 'a good death' would seem to be alien to a belief in which God is sovereign in a person's life. Euthanasia, which has been described as referring to death in which more direct intervention is involved, can be contrasted with physician-assisted suicide (PAS), when life is ended through the obtaining of a lethal dose prescription from a physician for the purpose of ending one's own life.[35] Researchers argue for a distinction between PAS and euthanasia, perhaps seeing PAS as a preferred *modus operandi*.[36] However, both seem to place the determination of life into the hands of the individual as a matter of choice, whether that choice is actively made and enacted by the individual in the case of PAS or made through the actions of others and the individual in the euthanasia scenario.

---

[35] A helpful article contrasting euthanasia with physician-assisted suicide (PAS) has been produced in L.A. Roscoe, J.E. Malphurs, L.J. Dragovic and D. Cohen, 'A Comparison of Characteristics of Kevorkian Euthanasia Cases and Physician Assisted Suicides in Oregon', *The Gerontologist* Vol. 41 No. 4 (The Gerontological Society of America, 2001), pp. 439–46.

[36] Ibid. PAS has been legalized in the state of Oregon.

At a recent conference the priest and gerontologist Elizabeth MacKinlay asked the question: 'What do we think when someone older suicides – what response does the community have?' Her answer was that all too often society thinks that because someone is old it is all right to take one's own life, like Seneca's heartfelt statement that he would rather take his own life than have it taken from him by old age. I remember visiting one older woman who resided in a nursing home. Her husband had died some time before, her eyesight had failed, she had little or no family, and each time the minister of her church and I visited she would say that she wanted to die. I am sure that there are many who have found themselves in the position of being asked by a beloved older person suffering the debilitating affects of age and illness to help them to end his or her life. To believe in a sovereign God is to trust that the length of our days is not to be determined by ourselves or others, but by him and him alone. These are hard words, and in practice, when faced with a suffering person, what should our compassionate response be? As a Christian I do not consider euthanasia or assisted suicide to be examples of 'good death' when facing illness in older age. However, in practice I have found myself praying for the release of the older person from suffering through death. A practical response I can make spiritually as a minister is in my own prayers to petition God to call the person to himself, to the place where there will be no more pain and where every tear of suffering will be wiped away.

Elder Abuse

Elder abuse as an identifiable phenomenon is relatively new in the UK, though this is not to suggest that elder abuse never occurred prior to its recognition. Like child abuse, and more latterly adult abuse, elder abuse has taken time to appear on research and public policy agendas. However, the church continues to be slow to recognize elder abuse, which is remarkable considering the amount of contact the average minister has with vulnerable older people in comparison to many other professions.

The organization Action on Elder Abuse (AEA) has defined elder abuse as 'A single or repeated act or lack of appropriate action occurring within any relationship where there is an expectation of trust which causes harm or distress to an older person.' AEA has identified the five following main types of abuse: physical, psychological, financial, sexual and neglect.[37] It established a confidential helpline that in two years received 1421 calls. In an analysis of calls AEA found that abuse increased with age, three times as many calls reported women being abused, and over a quarter of calls identified care workers as the abuser.

This is only the tip of the iceberg, as many vulnerable older people cannot make contact with such a helpline in order to find assistance in abusive situations. According to the recent government publication *No Secrets* a vulnerable adult is someone who:

> is or may be in need of community care services by reason of mental or other disability, age or illness; and who is or may be unable to take care of him or herself, or unable

---

[37] See the Action on Elder Abuse web site at < www.elder abuse.org >. If you would like further help or assistance contact AEA at Action on Elder Abuse, Astral House, 1268 London Road, London SW16 4ER, UK. Telephone: 0208 764 7648; e-mail: < aea@ace.org.uk >.

to protect him or herself against significant harm or ex-
ploitation.[38]

Churches and ministers need to be equipped to identify
abusive situations and to know how to seek assistance on
behalf of a vulnerable older person. But it is surprising
how resistant some churches can be to such a development. A few years ago a research project into identifying
ministers' awareness of elder abuse and responses to
it was prevented because the churches involved feared
that unfortunate headlines could come from the work! I
continue to find such a response incredible: a willingness
to ignore and a failure to protect or not accept the needs of
vulnerable older people is a rejection of God's expectation
of his people in the care of the older person. More than
this, when we stand by and ignore or fail to understand
abuse, we actually contribute to the continuing abuse of
the person.

The End of the Tour

This brief tour of the territory our pioneers are currently
crossing has only touched on a few issues. Others that
could be considered are the older person as the victim of
crime, issues of security, the experience of loneliness,[39] the

---

[38] *No Secrets: The Protection of Vulnerable Adults* (The Department
of Health, March 2000). See p. 7 for definition of vulnerable
adults. Copies of the report can be viewed at < www.doh.
gov.uk/scg/nosecrets.htm >.

[39] A recent and helpful study on this subject has been published by
H.B. Gibson, *Loneliness in Later Life* (Macmillan, 2000), which
questions the assumption that the experience of loneliness in
later life is normal and negative for the older person. Gibson's
research suggests an alternative understanding of loneliness as

increasing prevalence of depression due to retirement, and loss of role or mobility through illness.[40] There are other issues that may cause some surprise, for example, an increase in sexually transmitted diseases (STDs) amongst the over 65s, with some STDs increasing at a faster rate amongst older people than younger generations.[41] In America an increasing number of older people are committing gun crimes due to mental disorders associated with age.[42] In the UK the Home Office has forecasted a growth in crime committed by older people, as early retirement and longevity may cause 'a perceived lack of a constructive role in society. Just as with any other socially excluded group, this might lead to crime.'[43] If anything, this tour should have helped in the realization that older people are not some homogenous group for whom the experience of ageing is always the same. The silent revolution of age has been taking place all around us. But what does the future hold for future generations of older people?

[39] *(continued)* being received into the experience of the individual and therefore understood by older people in different ways.

[40] T. Macnair, *Elderly People and Depression*, BBC Online, 26 October 2000 at < www.bbc.co.uk/health/features/depression_elderly.shtml > (accessed 2 October 2001).

[41] T. Stuttaford, 'STDs – Sex and the Sixties', *The Times*, 10 July 2001. It must be noted that the rapid percentage increase of STDs amongst over 65s appears more dramatic because of the low numbers from which this increase began.

[42] I. Brodie, 'America's Elderly fill Sunset Days with Crime', *The Times*, 24 October 2000.

[43] R. Ford, 'Identity Thieves are a Threat to your Future', *The Times*, 25 March 2000, p. 12.

2

The Changing Scene

Never in human history has a population so wilfully and deliberately defied nature as has the present generation. How have we defied it? We have survived. Our unprecedented survival has produced a revolution in longevity which is shaking the foundations of societies around the world and profoundly altering our attitudes to life and death.[1]

The 2001 Reith Lecture series by Professor Tom Kirkwood focused on the issue of an ageing population. In his initial scene-setting lecture Kirkwood identified how attitudes to life and death are being profoundly altered. The implication of these altering attitudes to longevity means that, while the tour of issues in Chapter 1 can help in understanding the needs of current older generations, the revolution of age is bringing rapid

---

[1] Opening paragraph from the 2001 Reith Lecture 'Brave Old World' by Professor T. Kirkwood. Texts of each lecture are available at < www.bbc.co.uk/radio4/reith2001/.> Alternatively, the 2001 Reith Lectures have been published: T. Kirkwood, *The End of Age: Why Everything about Ageing is Changing* (Profile, 2001).

change as new generations age and bring into their own older age new experiences, expectations and issues.

But how easily are these diverging older generations identified? One of the difficulties when we start thinking of older people is that this segment of the population suddenly starts to become one large amorphous blob, lacking distinction or boundaries. The danger is simply that we can unwittingly start to see age as being static. Consider for a moment an older person. What kind of image comes into your mind, what activities do you consider an older person might enjoy? Do you think of an old-time sing-a-long or dancing, a luncheon club or social activity? A recent survey from the Christian Research Association highlighted the importance of the BBC television programme *Songs of Praise* for older people – approximately five million people tune in each week to watch it. Many of those viewers are from older generations.

The key question is this. Are these activities culturally relevant for *all* older people or for a couple of generations? Recent years have seen an increasing urgency in the call for an emphasis on reaching younger people, which has focused many churches' attentions on the issue of culture. We are called upon to be 'culturally relevant' to differing generations of younger people. But is the same true of our response to differing generations of older people? The previous chapter looked briefly at some of the issues facing older people today, but what of older people tomorrow? Our generations of older people are breaking new ground; they are not remaining static.

In the UK the present Labour government's major policy initiative of listening to older people has been entitled *Life Begins at 50: A Better Society for Older People*. In the opening section the Prime Minister, Tony Blair, makes the following observation:

I'm pleased that the saying 'life begins at 50' has been chosen as the title of this report. By updating the old phrase, it highlights both the remarkable increase in life expectancy and the fact that these extra years of life are, for most of us, both active and healthy. It means the old stereotypes about age – about who could or should do what, and when – are now meaningless. It's something which older people themselves have long recognised. But the rest of society has not always been as fast to understand these changes. And it is the old-fashioned attitudes of society as a whole which are now seen by many older people as one of the biggest remaining barriers to them fulfilling their potential and living life to the full. It is these remaining barriers, and these attitudes, which this Government is determined to take a lead in tackling.[2]

If any of us have had any preconceptions about older people and their expectations this statement will – hopefully – have just blown them away. It is older people themselves who are now challenging societal expectations of what it means to be older. If you think to be older means joining the five million who watch *Songs of Praise*, then you are failing to understand generational change. If older age begins at 50, as far as government policy in the UK is concerned, the church is facing the urgent need to be culturally relevant to a diverse population of older people, ranging from the baby boomers who experienced the massive societal shifts of the 1960s to those now in their fourth age who lived and served during the Second World War.

---

[2] Tony Blair's Foreword to *Life Begins at 50: A Better Society for Older People*, produced by the Department of Social Security Inter-Ministerial Group for Older People, May 2000.

The Breaking of Faith

Callum Brown's recent book *The Death of Christian Britain*[3] offers a way in which this distinctiveness between older generations can be identified and located historically. Brown provides an effective critique of the theory of secularization, which for many years has dominated discussion of the decline of the church in the Western world. Secularization is the term some sociologists have used to describe the impact of modern culture upon traditional religious institutions. Hence we hear and read about the 'decline of the traditional church'. David Martin, a sociologist of religion who wrote what is perhaps to be considered the standard work on secularization, saw this process of secularization taking place over a period of between two and four centuries, during which religious institutions became less powerful and religious beliefs were gradually less easily accepted.[4]

Brown's contribution has been to re-examine the historical, statistical and published data upon which this steady decline has been based, reaching the conclusion that for many years religious institutions and beliefs in the UK were remarkably well located within popular culture. In the nineteenth century evangelical publishing houses produced the first women's and girls' magazines, which were to prove very popular. In the twentieth century, Brown describes the 1950s as 'the last Victorian decade', with revival rallies during which 2 million people in London and 1.2 million people in Glasgow heard Billy Graham preach.[5] He observes that:

---

[3] C.G. Brown, *The Death of Christian Britain* (Routledge, 2001).
[4] D. Martin, *A General Theory of Secularisation* (Blackwell, 1978), p. 15.
[5] Brown, *The Death of Christian Britain*, pp. 5–6.

> The late 1940s and 1950s witnessed the greatest church growth that Britain had experienced since the mid-nineteenth century ... Some scholars miss its scale or even its existence ... Most, however, have ignored it because it does not fit their theoretical presumption that secularisation was underway long before, and that Britain was then a secular society.[6]

This scholarly discourse from sociological and historical debate has spilled over into theological discussion and training, so that many in positions of responsibility in our churches continue to examine church decline, develop responses and consider prevailing culture in the light of academic thought, which says this has been happening for centuries. We therefore accept the inevitability of decline rather than rising to the challenge of the break between Christianity and popular culture as recent a phenomenon of the last four decades.

Brown rejects the gradual decline of religion over centuries, placing his thesis firmly in the 1960s. It is from this point that he identifies the explosive growth of secularism:

> Whereas previously, men and women were able to draw upon a Christian-centred culture to find guidance about how they should behave, and how they should think about their lives, from the 1960s a suspicion of creeds arose that quickly took the form of a rejection of Christian tradition and all formulaic constructions of the individual.[7]

Brown provides a thorough analysis in support of his assertions, a broad description of which would be his iden-tification of both female and male alienation from religion,

---

[6] Ibid. p. 170.
[7] Ibid. p. 193.

the rise of ethical concerns dominating moral culture such as environmentalism, gender and racial equality, nuclear weapons and power and so on, combined with the rise of the individual rejecting conventional religious culture.[8] This leads to his observation of our present condition that 'At the start of the third millennium, we in Britain are in the midst of secularisation.'[9] This is not well-trodden territory that we are passing over in this brief analysis – it is brand new ground not broken before, which our pioneers of the third age are learning how to navigate. Perhaps the defining point in Brown's analysis is an observation from his own childhood in 1970s Edinburgh when large numbers of youth, including himself, were part of a church hall circuit of rock dances and discos. However, congregations unable to accept the increasing loudness of the music, the issue of drugs, police visits and teenagers' casual sexual liaisons shut this down. For Brown this was when 'the salvation industry was shutting its doors to an entire generation of youngsters who no longer subscribed to religious discourses of moral identity. Secularisation was now well under way … The religious alienation of the next generation of children followed.'[10]

If Brown's thesis is correct, and I am increasingly convinced that it is, then it has tremendous implications for the church in the UK and the rest of the world. In this silent revolution of age we are in the midst of the generational breakage between those who were the adult generations of the 1950s and prior and those who have grown and developed during and after the 1960s. The implication of this breakage is that we can no longer

---

[8] Ibid. See Chapter 8, The 1960s and Secularisation, for the detail of Brown's argument.

[9] Ibid.

[10] Ibid. pp. 180, 192.

assume that future generations of older people will automatically return to the church as part of their process of
ageing. Future older generations rejected Christianity
and the church in their youth; they have grown and
developed without it and seem happy to continue that
way. These are people now in their 50s and demanding a
very different view of ageing from society, let alone from a
church that has little to say on the subject. We in institutional Christianity have become caught up in these
younger older people's desire to focus on the attributes of
youth, to live out the very best quality of life now, not
later. We are failing to discover the significance of older
age and failing to invest time, energy and resources in
telling these new older people about Jesus in ways that
are culturally appropriate for their generation, not only
for the generation of their parents.

This generational process of secularization is not
limited to the UK. It has been experienced in varying
degrees within the Western world as a whole, and
appears to be increasingly evident in other cultures.
Anecdotal evidence from a two-month trip to Malaysia in
2000 demonstrated to me the divide beginning to occur
in spirituality and spiritual awareness of older and
younger members of Malay society, particularly amongst
the Chinese community. Where once spiritual affiliations
other than Christianity were of paramount importance
to family, there was the beginning of a breakdown
in adherence, which was by all accounts a more recent
phenomenon.

Further, there are more recent statistical examples of
this rupture between generations that has taken place. A
recent MORI poll on behalf of the Evangelical Alliance in
the UK, conducted as part of an ongoing research project
into the social impact of Christian churches and organizations, produced interesting results when respondents

were identified according to age.[11] Survey participants were asked the following question: 'How important a role, if at all, do you think Christian churches and groups play in speaking out on social issues in Britain today?' Of the responses grouped into 'important' they broke down according to age in the following way: 16–24 = 31 per cent, 25–34 = 30 per cent, 35–44 = 36 per cent, 45–54 = 36 per cent, 55–64 = 47 per cent, and 65+ = 54 per cent. The survey doesn't allow us to see variations according to age beyond 65+, but there is a fascinating difference among the generations. Between 65+ and 55–64 we can see a 7 per cent difference in the number of people who considered Christian churches and groups played an important role in speaking out on social issues, but between 65+ and 45–54, that difference extends to 18 per cent!

In the space of a couple of age brackets not that far apart you see the implication of generational differences. These differences fit acknowledged patterns that one would expect to see: older generations desiring, to some degree, to hear the voice of the church in a clearer promotion of moral values (though this was only 54 per cent of respondents over 65); and younger generations who do not consider the church's role to be 'speaking out' to society. However, when we speak of 'younger generations' this includes those who are over 50, and in the group Tony Blair described as challenging the expectations of ageing as they themselves grow older.

---

[11] I am most grateful to the Revd John S. Smith, UK Director of the Evangelical Alliance, for the use of this yet unpublished research. The survey, entitled 'The Role of Christian Churches and Groups in Society', was conducted by MORI Social Research in March 2002.

Into the Future

Having suggested that we cannot expect from future older generations the same attitude and cultural expectations towards the process of ageing as previous older generations, we need to consider how these new expectations of age may affect people. Therefore, as we look towards the future we will consider the impact of older consumers, the customization of age, and the influence of older people with both increased wealth and increased power in society. These older people will increasingly hold positions of influence in our society and in our churches simply by their numerical and economic resources.

However, there is one further slice of recent social theory that needs to be included, as it provides the foundation for our looking towards the future of older age. Many commentators have acknowledged the rise of the individual in society; the sociologist Zygmunt Bauman in his recent book *The Individualized Society* has produced a helpful exploration of the individualization of society. In his final chapter Bauman asks the question 'Is there life after immortality?' and examines the way in which people are increasingly unconcerned about any form of afterlife. Bauman suggests that the ultimate experience of life has become death itself, for death is no longer a passage to anything else:[12]

> The ancient slogan *carpe diem* has acquired an altogether different sense and carries a new message: collect your credits now – thinking of tomorrow is a waste of time. The culture of credit cards has replaced the culture of savings accounts.[13]

---

[12] Z. Bauman, *The Individualized Society* (Polity, 2001), p. 247.
[13] Ibid.

Bauman's observations provide a tremendous insight into the rapidly changing picture already identified. The ever-increasing pressure from ageing generations is for life now, not later. People are no longer satisfied to accept ill health or a low quality of life. The concern is to 'collect your credits now'. Commenting on our credit card economy and lifestyles, Bauman makes the following vital statement: 'Credit cards were introduced into general use two decades ago under the slogan "take the waiting out of wanting".'[14]

The phenomenon and effect of consumerism is not new; the life of credit has existed for over twenty years, and those who were the first users of such facilities are those generations who are now approaching their third age. These older credit generations carry with them a desire not to save but to consume, as no longer do they see anything lying beyond death. The connection of religion and popular culture that their parents experienced no longer exists. Bauman rightly notes that most people have always wanted their life to be longer and would do whatever they could to put off death itself, but, as he observes:

> hardly ever has the urge to fight death back played such a central role in shaping life strategies and life's purposes as it does today. A long life, a fit life – the kind of life which allows the consumption of all the pleasures life has to offer – is today the supreme value and the principal objective of life efforts. For this new hierarchy of values the technology of cloning comes in handy: in the age of spare parts it brandishes the prospect of making replaceable the most precious part of them all …[15]

---

[14] Ibid.
[15] Ibid. p. 248.

One of the most remarkable figures in the effort to fight death is the Texan oil millionaire Miller Quarles, who has committed his wealth to fund research aimed not only at prolonging life, but defying death itself. The initial momentum for this came from his concern to prolong his own life, to put off that moment of death, after which there would appear to be nothing for many people today: no heaven, no hell – simply no existence. A recent BBC documentary profiled the life of this man who exemplifies the credit card culture of current generations of older people. Following an extraordinary fitness regime, an exact diet and taking vitamin supplements, Quarles has sought to buy extra time to enable science to catch up with his desire to continue living.[16] One may criticize this man's use of his wealth, his spending his way into eternity. However, when there is no such thing as hope; when death is all there is; when God seems irrelevant; when the church has no way of reaching out; then this life is all there is. Death is the word that dare not be mentioned. During a degree course seven years ago I watched a documentary about a retirement community in Florida. Here, older people lived in ideally designed homes, with beautiful grounds and surroundings, the golf course was simply an electric buggy ride away, and gyms and shops were close at hand. The aim of this community was purely to satisfy the demands of life, but it had no way of celebrating death or even acknowledging death's existence. When a member of this community died in their home, the funeral directors would come at night to remove the body, so that no one would see death pass by them in the form of the black hearse, and remarkably people were not mentioned after

---

[16] Miller Quarles was profiled in the BBC's *Horizon* programme, broadcast on BBC2 at 8.00 p.m. on Tuesday 4 January 2000.

their death. They no longer existed in life or in memory – death was the end.

These credit card generations are creating new rules for life, new strategies, and have new expectations. There has never been a time like this, in which we are witnessing older generations of people becoming consuming generations, driven by the desire to live life now, to achieve a satisfactory quality of life and to 'seize the day', for there is nothing past death to be seized.

Older Consumers

In a UK context, the best example of the advent of the older consumer is the continual and rapid growth of the company Saga, which now provides a wide range of services to people aged over 50. As generations have aged and become new consumers of Saga's services it has been possible to witness a change in attitudes. A decade ago Saga was associated with older people on coach holidays. Today one can watch adverts for the newly launched Saga radio station and look on the Saga web site for the latest cruise information and holiday offers – you can even listen to Saga Radio as you surf the web site![17] Recent television advertising for Saga Radio focused on a boy listening to rock and roll, wearing a short-sleeved T-shirt, and polishing the chrome hub of one of the wheels of his first car. The fascinating nature of this advert was twofold: first, it aimed to appeal to the generation now over 50, who were culturally distinct from their parents' generation; and second, it was a direct appeal back to youth. Other examples are two recent cover photos for *Saga Magazine*.[18] One

---

[17] Go to < www.saga.co.uk >.
[18] *Saga Magazine* is designed for the over-50s market.

showed the 1960s model Twiggy, whilst another showed a picture of Mick Jagger. Both are icons of the post-war generation, which, as one couple said to me recently, was the first generation of teenagers, distinct in their fashion and music tastes from any generation before them.[19] Perhaps the paradox is that one of the icons of this post-war generation, which broke with their parents' generation, is now established with the title 'Sir' Mick Jagger. The web site of *Saga Magazine* reports its circulation as approximately one million, with a readership of two million.[20] A recent article from the magazine made available via the Saga web site was entitled 'Older Models ... Faces of the Present', which quoted the manager of a leading London model agency as saying, 'Society is kicking back after all those years of supermodels. There's a feeling, "Let's have some models who represent what's actually going on."'[21]

There are two important trends in understanding 'what's actually going on': first, the issue of this section, the rise of consumer culture; second, the rise of the third age as the age of personal fulfilment. The gerontologist Andrew Blaikie observes that these two trends combine to create an ageing population that stimulates market demand for leisure and lifestyle services and products.[22] Many older people will not share in the experience of being an active participant in these older consumer generations. There will remain a significant number of older people who live in poverty, facing increased risk in health and personal security. Despite this disparity of experience

---

[19] A. Blaikie, *Ageing and Popular Culture* (Cambridge University Press, 1999), p. 107.

[20] Figures taken from the *Saga Magazine* web site.

[21] E. Tromans, 'Older Models ... Faces of the Present', *Saga Magazine*, April 2002.

[22] Blaikie, *Ageing and Popular Culture*, p. 107.

there is an identifiable trend of an expanding market being created by older consumers. But the question remains: why is this trend happening? The following section will look at possible answers to this question, but there is one final comment to be added before suggesting any form of answer. In a newspaper interview in 1993 Mick Jagger observed: 'People have this obsession ... They want you to be like you were in 1969. They want you to, because otherwise their youth goes with you, you know?'[23] The desire to sustain youth either through images or the continuing existence of celebrities would seem to be a powerful aphrodisiac for many who are willing to expend resources on the products and services necessary to supposedly stave off old age. Each day we are presented with television advertisements to halt the signs of ageing – creams that promise, through 'exclusive formulas', to provide a surface-covering veneer of youth. But is this what people truly want? Surely there cannot be that many people who want old age to become a 'caricature of youth culture'?[24]

In this world, with its increasing number of older consumers, the church has an opportunity to enable people to see the actual value of older age. It can help them see past the facial cream that only satisfies the outward demand for youth and enable them to meet with the God who looks upon the inward condition of the heart. But to do this the church needs to be culturally relevant and aware of the needs of these new older generations. It must not pander to the demand for consumption and the maintenance of youth, but celebrate older age. The mask of surface youth is unsustainable and people will experience a fourth age with its heightened risk of ill health and

---

[23] Quote from the *Observer Magazine* in ibid. p. 107.
[24] Ibid. p. 108.

frailty. In the struggles of both the third and fourth ages the church has an opportunity to speak of the promises of Christ Jesus. Eternal life is not about struggling to maintain what we have now, fighting against the supposed threat of age and ultimately of the greatest thief of all – death. Eternal life is about embracing the hope and promise of the life to come in Christ, and joining with St Paul in the question, 'Where, O death, is your victory? Where, O death, is your sting?' (1 Corinthians 15:55). An older member of the church in which I serve recently died. Shortly before her death she shared with a Bible study group the Christian reality of ageing and death (2 Corinthians 4:16,18):

> we do not lose heart. Though outwardly we are wasting away, yet inwardly we are being renewed day by day … So we fix our eyes not on what is seen, but on what is unseen. For what is seen is temporary, but what is unseen is eternal.

Customization

The trend of customization has been described as the 'second consumer revolution' whereby businesses are increasingly tailoring products to suit the demands of individuals or groups of customers.[25] One need only consider the supermarket loyalty card schemes in the UK that are able to track your purchases and identify special offers that would suit you. Or think of the Internet bookshops that track your purchase patterns and then make specific book recommendations the next time you log on to their site. The impact of such a consumer revolution is

---

[25] M. Moynagh, *Changing World, Changing Church* (Monarch, 2001), p. 19.

to highlight and reinforce the growing individualization of society.[26] This revolution isn't only youth driven. It has its origins in the generations that demanded something different, that were the first to use credit cards, which were to embrace new phenomena from rock and roll music to package holidays!

When one examines Internet usage in the UK the age category with the majority of users is younger people: 82 per cent of those aged 16–24 have accessed the Internet at some time, in contrast to 16 per cent of those over 65. These are hardly surprising results between vastly different generations. More significant are the differences between generations of older people themselves: 31 per cent of those aged 55–64 and 54 per cent of those aged 45–54 have accessed the Internet at some time.[27] When compared to the original 16 per cent of those over 65, we see generations who are ageing and expressing different patterns and methods of consumption, which emphasize the priority of the consumer in the act of consumption. The development of customization has simply taken the information held about people in today's technological society and applied it to the 'benefit' of the consumer. Michael Moynagh identifies the issue for the church as he explores the way in which churches have retained the 'one-size-fits-all' mindset of what the church should be. He observes: 'The church could get away with it in mass society, but in an it-must-fit-me world it won't wash anymore.'[28] In this 'it-must-fit-me' world the older consumer is increasingly

---

[26] R. Merchant, 'Cell Church: Culturally Appropriate?' in M. Green (ed.), *Church Without Walls: A Global Examination of Cell Church* (Paternoster, 2002).

[27] 'Internet Access June 2001' issued by National Statistics Office, London. See p. 7 of the report for access according to age.

[28] Ibid. p. 33.

becoming the most important market sector. Peter Drucker, an expert in organizational culture and management studies, has observed: 'The youth market is over. It's an old rule that the population group that is the biggest and growing fastest determines the mood ...'[29] It is therefore amazing that many churches, as observed in Chapter 1, have no mission statement or strategy that offers any priority to the needs of older people, when these are increasingly enfranchised generations. It is even more remarkable when one considers the significant numbers of older people who form part of the church in the UK. Perhaps it is that these older generations who wish to maintain youth and so delay the realities of older age are more concerned to reach younger people, as youth does not challenge them as much as their own process of growing older.

Increased Wealth

The existence of a developing divide between rich and poor older people has already been mentioned. However, the extent of this growing divide and the implication of increased wealth is remarkable. The *Investors Chronicle* carried an article in 2001 called 'Tomorrow's World', drawing together information from a number of different sources examining the impact of an ageing population upon the life and wallet of investors. It observed that the market research firm Mintel predicted that over the following five years 55–59 year olds would be the fastest-growing sector of the population, increasing by 22 per

---

[29] W.D. Novelli, 'The Social Dimension of Sustainable Development' at < www.aarp.org/intl/speech.html > (accessed 14 May 2002).

cent. Noting the decreasing number of traditional family units, the article observed that in the UK in 1996 there were 5.8 million single-person households. By 2020 house builders are predicting 8.4 million single-person households, with this number having been swollen by the increased number of retired people living on their own, either because they never married or because a relationship ended. In the US similar changes in the age make-up of consumers are taking place: the majority of new cars sold to non-corporate purchasers were sold to retirees. Returning to the UK, the influence of generations who were the first to purchase package holidays can be further seen in the current overseas holiday market, where the over-45s make up 44 per cent, and this is only expected to increase.[30] These financially resourced older members of the population have been given the acronym 'Woopies' – meaning 'well-off older people'![31] One commentator drawing on a 1994 report from the Henley Centre drew the following picture of a future with 'Woopies':

> The first mass leisure class in history is on its way … It will be made up of people aged between 50–75 who have more free time and money, and higher expectations than their predecessors and were brought up to value aspiration and self-fulfilment. The 'Third-Agers' of tomorrow, now in their forties, represent a decisive break from the past … Unlike preceding generations whose up-bringing gave them a more frugal outlook, they were socialised in the 1960s, 'a decade

---

[30] V. Tkach, 'Tomorrow's World', *Investors Chronicle* Vol. 137/ 1745 (Financial Times Business 17–23 August 2001), pp. 26–8.

[31] C. Jardine, 'Woopie', first published in *The Telegraph* in November 1994, quoted in C. Donnellan (ed.), *Our Ageing Generation* Vol. 16 (Independence, 1995), p. 5.

of expanding individual choices and apparently inherent economic growth'.[32]

Predicting the future wealth of older populations is not an exact science. Financial growth, recession, property boom and bust, government legislation on retirement, the end of the guaranteed final income pension, immigration policy (some commentators suggest increased immigration could carry the shortfall in the UK's numbers of younger people to support an ageing population through taxation) – all of these factors are ultimately unknowns.

But what can be reasonably identified is evidence that suggests the increasing financial power of older generations and their willingness to consume in ways different from previous generations. An implication of wealth and numerical influence that we may be certain of is the change in the power structure of the population in the UK, which is already evident.

Increased Power

The rise in 'grey power' was perhaps most potently seen after the defeat of the Labour Party in local council elections in 2000 when *The Times* newspaper titled an article 'Blair Urged to Buy Back the Pensioner Vote'. *The Times* contacted 150 Labour Party councillors who had lost their council seats. When asked why they felt they had lost their seats, 117 of the 150 (78 per cent) ex-councillors replied that they lost primarily because of anger over pensions. (The government had announced a rise of 75 pence per

---

[32] D. Nicholson-Lord, 'Mass Leisure Class is on the Way, say Forecasters', first published in *The Independent* in April 1994, quoted in Donnellan, *Our Ageing Generation*, p. 34.

week in pensions in that year's budget, which was denounced as derisory by pensioner action groups.)[33] A similar article, once again in *The Times*, was carried a year later in the build-up to the 2001 general election, and highlighted the twin issues for older people: the amount of state pension received and how much older people pay for care in older age:

> The grey vote is vital to the fortunes of all three parties. Pensioner power embarrassed the Government throughout its first term ... A survey by MORI and Help the Aged found that 15% of voters with a preferred party would be 'very likely' to switch to another that promised free personal care. In addition, 54% of floating voters said the issue would influence their decision.[34]

In a society in which we are seeing younger voters becoming apathetic towards the political process, be assured that older people are more likely to use their vote. More importantly, there are only increasing numbers of older people in the electorate, who, as the above survey observed, are beginning to realize their political power. Quite how homogenous this power will be is uncertain. It is doubtful that somehow older people will 'gang together' to ensure their own political agenda to the detriment of younger voters. However, it is likely that we will see older people uniting around single-issue campaigns, such as pensions or the cost of residential care, in order to put their views forward. And we are likely to see political parties seeking to capture the 'grey vote' simply because

---

[33] J. Landale, L. Peek and G. Jacob, 'Blair Urged to Buy Back the Pensioner Vote', *The Times*, 15 May 2000.

[34] A. Senior and C. Stewart, 'Promises with a Silver Lining', *The Times*, 19 May 2001.

of the ever-increasing number of older people, who tend to be more politically aware and active.

In America the rise of 'gray power' has already been well documented, as the post-war baby boom generation occurred a decade earlier than in the UK, where post-war austerity measures remained in place until the late 1950s. In the USA in 1991 the Association for Retired Persons over 50 (AARP) claimed to have 125,000 members[35] and in a recent speech by AARP's Chief Executive Officer, William D. Novelli, the 2002 membership was stated as 35.2 million.[36] The principle aims of AARP have been documented as changing attitudes to age, ending age discrimination in employment (including compulsory retirement) and equalizing ages at which men and women become eligible for pensions and associated benefits.[37] One the most remarkable examples from the USA of the political influence of older people, which is yet to be seen in the UK, has been AARP's lobbying during the recent presidential elections. Through provision of a voter express bus and sponsorship of presidential and vice-presidential debates, AARP claimed to have brought social security, Medicare and prescription drug provision to the centre of each party's election platform.[38]

---

[35] J. Ginn, 'Grey Power: Age-based Organisations' Response to Structured Inequalities', *Critical Social Policy* 38, Autumn 1993, p. 33.

[36] Novelli, 'The Social Dimension of Sustainable Development' at < www.aarp.org/intl/speech.html >.

[37] Ginn, 'Grey Power', p. 33.

[38] AARP 2000 Annual Report, 'Your Choice, Your Voice, Your Attitude', available in pdf format from < www.aarp.org/ar/ 2000 >.

The Aphrodisiac of Power

As we look into the future there are many differing variables that need to be held in tension. The next chapter will begin the process of uncovering the role and value of the older person – and old age – in God's purposes. The phenomenon of grey power is taking place in a society experiencing ever-increasing individualization. This is something that not only academics but more importantly older people themselves are realizing. One of the most thought-provoking presentations of this realization of power that I have seen was a cartoon strip called 'Him and Her' in a newspaper magazine. The cartoon was titled 'Her Mother and Him Discuss Age Discrimination' and contained the following conversation:

Mother: We have the experience ...

Him: Yes ...

Mother: of being pampered physically (NHS), intellectually (free university education), and economically (job tenure, career structure, life-time contract, job with prospects) ... and we don't want to give it up.

3

Ageing in the Old Testament

The theologian J. Gordon Harris has rightly observed that biblical material in general lacks a systematic theology of ageing.[1] However, fine threads of the role and experience of the older person do run through the biblical text, and these threads are intricately interwoven within God's plans. The need to recover the uniqueness of the biblical portrait of older people is an urgent task, as this portrait stands not only in contrast to the world in which we now live, but provides a record to a historic witness of contrast and reveals God's purposes for the older person.

Caution needs to be shown when using material from antiquity. References to old age are few, but they enable us to see the impression of and reaction to old age and older people by writers for their intended audiences.[2] Such references suggest that often in antiquity older people were a point of fear and derision. The philosopher Seneca saw old age as a threat, and if it were to 'shatter my mind, and to

---

[1] J. Gordon Harris, *God and the Elderly* (Fortress Press, 1987). This observation by Gordon Harris forms the conclusion to the preface.

[2] T. Parkin, 'Ageing in Antiquity: Status and Participation' in P. Johnson and P. Thane (eds), *Old Age from Antiquity to Postmodernity* (Routledge, 1998), p 21.

pull its various faculties to pieces, if it leaves me, not life, but only the breath of life, I shall leap from a building that is crumbling and tottering'.[3] The fifth-century Greek anthologist Joannes Stobaeus's collection of writings, dating from the seventh century BC to the fourth century AD, bring together a variety of references on old age. While some of the collected material is in praise of old age, many of the writings provide negative portrayals. There are lengthy attacks upon the aged in areas of physical disability, illness, loss of pleasures and senses, fear of death, impotence, the ridicule of younger generations, exclusion from political and military affairs, and particularly the problem of poverty in old age.[4] Such negative views increased significantly in the case of women: if they were past the age of menopause, and therefore no longer able to fulfil duties as reproducers, elderly women were often portrayed as brothel madams, witches or alcoholics.[5]

The contrast of the Old Testament witness to these negative portrayals is clear. The integration of all aspects of life in the Hebraic world meant that honour was to be accorded to the person who attained old age, as a long life was considered a sign of God's blessing.[6] Old age was also viewed positively because it was believed that persons of great age had acquired knowledge and wisdom that could benefit others, and if the Israelite society was largely illiterate, then older people were the main source of oral history and tradition.[7] The biblical picture of ageing provides

---

[3] Ibid. p. 28.
[4] Ibid. p. 22.
[5] Ibid. p. 33.
[6] W.A. VanGemeren (ed.), *New International Dictionary of Old Testament Theology and Exegesis* Vol. 1 (Paternoster, 1997). See commentary note on p. 1136.
[7] Ibid.

images of respect, honour and the assurance that God will never abandon the older person for whom physical frailty was an ever-present threat. This is not to suggest that there are no negative portrayals of older age in the Bible. But often where one reads descriptions of the debilitating conditions of older age, such as that of Ecclesiastes 12:1–7, the graphic picture is used as an instrument to implore the reader to remember God before[8] 'the silver chord is severed, or the golden bowl is broken; before the pitcher is shattered at the spring, or the wheel broken at the well, and the dust returns to the ground it came from, and the spirit returns to the God who gave it' (verses 6–7).

This chapter will take a series of different images and people from the Old Testament, so beginning to explore the thread that exists in Scripture regarding older people. The intention is not to present a wholly positive portrait of the older person. A negative picture of old age is not something to be avoided, as it is often found in expressions of the reality of old age in antiquity. But the role of the older person as inspirer, leader, encourager, witness and so on needs to be revealed once again for the church today. This is not offered as a definitive list: I am sure that many will read the following pages and see either aspects of an image that have been missed or images missed out altogether. However, this list is offered to stimulate thought, response and application.

Abraham and Sarah

Genesis 17:15–17 sees God's promise to Abraham. It is a wonderful assurance of covenant relationship expressed more fully in verse 19: 'Then God said, "Yes, but your wife

---

[8] Ibid.

Sarah will bear you a son, and you will call him Isaac. I will establish my covenant with him as an everlasting covenant for his descendants after him."' The remarkable aspect for both Abraham and Sarah is God's promise to accomplish this through a son. Abraham, speaking to himself in the quietness of his own thoughts, wondered (17:17) 'Will a son be born to a man a hundred years old? Will Sarah bear a child at the age of ninety?' Sarah repeats the same sentiment in the following chapter (18:12): 'After I am worn out and my master is old, will I now have this pleasure?' For both Abraham and Sarah their comments are spoken only to themselves, and with the laughter of disbelief. Yet in both cases the God who knows the thoughts of our hearts speaks into that which Abraham and Sarah thought was a private sphere. Walter Brueggemann observes that 'Abraham, and especially Sarah, are not offered here as models of faith but as models of disbelief. For them, the powerful promise of God outdistances their ability to receive it.'[9]

The immediacy of the frailty that older age had brought for both Abraham and Sarah distanced them from what they knew God could accomplish. Having been unable to conceive throughout the years when childbearing would be expected, God now declares to this older couple his intention to bring about what would otherwise be impossible. This wonderful story provides insight into the realities of older age. An older person becomes increasingly aware of the limitations advancing years bring, compensating, trying to except and dealing with the complications the lack of physical and mental health can bring. To put it simply, the experience of growing old brings with it for many the reality of physical limitation. However, into this story bursts the actual reality of God's sovereignty over all

---

[9] W. Brueggemann, *Genesis* (John Knox Press, 1982), p. 158.

things, including age, in the question 'Is anything too hard for the Lord?' (18:14). It is a timely reminder that even when faced with the apparent realities of older age there is still time for God because he is the God of all time and times. Brueggemann observes the power of the Lord's question to Sarah:

> To do the impossible! The gospel in this text reaches beyond our frames of reference. It breaks out of the parameters of reason, wisdom, morality, and common sense. It questions normal epistemology. It shatters accepted value systems. It is the heaviest criticism available about our definitions of reality.[10]

In this story God reveals his ability to change not only older people but also their life situations. Abraham and Sarah's disbelief had sprung out of their life experiences. It did not suddenly occur that day when God met with them – it was disbelief forged in life disappointment and dismissed with laughter that anything could change. For Abraham and Sarah, seeing the reality of God healing disappointment that had lasted over many years was to inspire lives in which faithfulness and trust was to follow.[11] How amazing it is that through this God provides a visible reminder of his covenant with Abraham, described in the opening of chapter 17, through his provision to this elderly couple of the child Isaac.

Naomi

The Old Testament also records points of affliction for the older person, as Naomi, in the book of Ruth, discovers

---

[10] Ibid. p. 159.
[11] See particularly the story of Isaac in Genesis 22:1–18.

when she finds herself with no husband and no sons to provide for her. Widowhood in antiquity often meant that with the death of a husband a woman became more vulnerable to old age.[12] In the book of Ruth the situation of Naomi is one of desperation. Her husband dead, her sons having also died leaving no children, she implores her daughters-in-law: 'Return home, my daughters; I am too old to have another husband. Even if I thought there was still hope for me – even if I had a husband tonight and gave birth to sons – would you wait until they grew up?' (1:12–13).

Naomi's vulnerability is all too apparent. The risks she faced as an older woman were to great for her to involve her daughters-in-law. However, to leave these passages here would be a mistake, for they reveal a great depth to the spirituality of the older person despite the afflictions that life may bring. This is a significant point, as the book of Ruth does not leave the older woman, Naomi, as the 'victim' of the piece. Rather, Naomi's prayer (1:8–9) demonstrates her own commitment to care for the two young women, Orpah and Ruth, and whilst Naomi acknowledges her suffering, she still refers to God in personal terms as 'Lord' and 'the Almighty' (1:20–21).

The theologian David Atkinson observes that the afflictions Naomi has faced cause her to bring her feelings before Yahweh; in fact she is to place the responsibility for her plight on Yahweh's shoulders:

His [Yahweh's] has been the hand behind the famine and the deaths first of her husband and then of her sons. Yet, she holds these bitter experiences in the setting of his covenant promises, by reminding herself and her daughter-in-law of

---

[12] Harris, *God and the Elderly*, p. 15.

his covenant name: Yahweh, the Lord ... Such a faith must have been a major influence on Ruth.[13]

In my own reading of this story I had often missed this vital observation; that the care Naomi was to receive from Ruth, so often the common understanding of this short book, was inspired by Naomi's care first. The key to Naomi's expression of care was rooted in this older woman's trust in the divine justice of God. Ultimately, the influence of Naomi upon Ruth is to be seen in Ruth's desire to remain with her mother-in-law to care for her, and Ruth's adoption of Naomi's faith identity: 'Your people will be my people and your God my God' (1:16). The conclusion to this story is brought about through Ruth's remarriage to a kinsman redeemer, who recognizes Ruth's care for her mother-in-law (2:11–12). The book of Ruth concludes with the recognition of the way in which Yahweh had provided for Naomi, and returns to the theme of Naomi's own care giving (4:14–16):

> The women said to Naomi: 'Praise be to the Lord, who this day has not left you without a kinsman-redeemer. May he become famous throughout Israel! He will renew your life and sustain you in your old age. For your daughter-in-law, who loves you and who is better to you than seven sons, has given him birth.' Then Naomi took the child, laid him in her lap and cared for him.

The book of Ruth provides a marvellous example of the interaction between an older and younger person. Remembering that women in antiquity often faced the greatest vulnerability, and that older women today still

---

[13] D. Atkinson, *The Message of Ruth* (Inter-Varsity Press, 1983), pp. 48–9.

face significant negative stereotyping, the implications of this story of Naomi and Ruth are significant to our own understanding. The provision of care, despite hardship, is paramount, rooted in the trust of God's divine justice in spite of present suffering: God will fulfil his promises to his people. The story recognizes the role of the older person not only as the recipient of care but also as the giver and inspirer of care. Yet the challenge of the story of Ruth is both to embrace the need to care for the older person at great personal cost and recognize the importance of the older person in the care of the wider family and the individual. This is not merely a confirmation of the role of the younger person to care for the older person; it is also the challenge to the older person to be an inspirer of care through his or her own life. It is a demonstration of the power of relationship that transcends the human-constructed boundaries of age through a mutual recognition and reliance upon God in each of these women's lives.

The interaction between Naomi and Ruth provides us with a powerful model of how an older women not only inspired but in many ways mentored a younger women. We see Naomi's desire to continue trusting God despite the situation in which she found herself to be combined with her concern for Ruth, and we see Ruth's willingness to be inspired by this older woman in her own life. It is a tremendous challenge and encouragement to us today to dare to take on this model, not dismissing the older person either as someone who represents by his or her appearance a fear of old age, or as someone who is no longer relevant, but instead as a person who has lived life with and through God and who can inspire the younger person to do the same.

Job

The story of Job, both detailed in its portrayal and compli-
cated to unravel, offers an insight into the tension between
a person's belief in God and personal experience.[14] The
major theme that runs throughout the story of Job is that of
the 'mystery of innocent suffering'.[15] David Atkinson
observes of the story of Job that: 'This book asks us to walk
with Job right through the depths of his struggle, open to
wherever he takes us, for only so will we catch the significance of the Lord's gracious voice at the journey's end.'[16]
This encouragement to walk with Job presents us with the
image of a journey, a path travelled through life, which
speaks of the life experience of the individual who has
trodden this journey. Job, an older and respected man,
presents us with an image of someone who has walked
faithfully during his life and yet is faced with extreme
physical suffering. Many of our pioneers of the third age
as they journey into their fourth age will be faced with the
experience of suffering in their lives.

The story of Job also provides insight into the respect
accorded to elders within Israelite society, for example in
12:12, where the writer states: 'Is not wisdom found among
the aged? Does not long life bring understanding?' This
verse provides a reminder of the idea found in Old Testament Scripture that the longer the person lived the wiser
they became. The older person, though, is not considered
to be the greatest source of wisdom: God is the oldest by far
and therefore he is certainly the wisest of all.[17] The context

---

[14] J.E. Hartley, *The Book of Job* (Eerdmans, 1988). See p. 43ff. for
Hartley's detailed outline of the story's major themes.

[15] D. Atkinson, *The Message of Job* (Inter-Varsity Press, 1991), p. 15.

[16] Ibid. p. 16.

[17] Hartley, *The Book of Job*, p. 213.

of this passage demonstrates the sovereignty of God's wisdom and ultimately the inadequacy of human wisdom, hence we read in 12:20 that 'He silences the lips of the trusted advisors and takes away the discernment of elders.'

The word 'elder' in the Old Testament tends to be used in two specific ways: first, to denote old age; second, as a term referring to a leader of the community. This second use of the word is attested to in ancient culture where older men were given authority and leadership because of the wisdom they had accumulated through their life experience. A sign of curse was to kill all the older men of a house so that their strength and wisdom were destroyed and so not available to the next generations (see Genesis 50:7; Psalm 105:22).[18] At a recent training morning for local ministers about the role of the older person in the church and society I heard a wonderful description of what it means to be aged. One minister described an older person who had been part of a congregation for a long time as someone who 'held the memories of the church'. But how easy it is in our present age to discount the memories of the older person as no longer relevant. We ask questions such as: 'What do they know of our world?' However, if we were to ask, many would find that the older person tends to know a great deal about the issues that we face in life, as these holders of memories have faced such issues themselves. The issues people face today are the same as those faced yesterday. Such is the nature of sin that it is evident in the experience of each generation and in every societal condition. The difference between the younger and older person is that we often use different descriptive words and images.

---

[18] VanGemeren, *New International Dictionary of Old Testament Theology and Exegesis* Vol. 1, p. 1134.

One the most wonderful things that happened to my wife and I when we joined the staff of the church in which we both currently serve was to be given an induction programme that included meeting various older members of the church community. It was a tremendous blessing to hear these people describe how God in his faithfulness had sustained the witness of the church amongst the local community. Hearing these memories of the church's life and wisdom shared gave us an insight into how the church had been one that had historically experienced and dealt with a great deal of change in its life. This knowledge has helped us as we have planned new programmes and looked to how we might best serve the church. The respect and honour of the elder is an aspect to be recovered in our lives – it is something to be enriched by and to learn from.

The story of Job does not provide us with a one-sided picture of elders who are only ever to be afforded respect. Yes, older men were to be honoured and young men were to demonstrate respect towards them, as seen in 32:4 where the writer describes how the young Elihu had waited before speaking because Job and his companions were older than he was. But as Elihu begins his series of speeches, which finally serve to prepare Job for God's appearing,[19] he makes the following observation in verses

---

[19] Hartley, *The Book of Job*, p. 430. Atkinson and Hartley differ in their interpretation of these four speeches by Elihu. Atkinson offers the view of Elihu who 'blusters on to the stage as an angry young man, full of his own importance' (Atkinson, *The Message of Job*, p. 122). However, this reading of the passage seems to be overly influenced by a modern Western understanding, which doesn't pick up the intricacy of relationship between young and old in antiquity. Whilst accepting the youthful bluster of Elihu, who does overstep the mark in his third speech, one tends to agree with Hartley's description of

8–9: 'But it is the spirit in a man, the breath of the Almighty, that gives him understanding. It is not only the old who are wise, not only the aged who understand what is right.' Here he challenges the traditional assumption that the aged are always wise by observing that the elders may not always understand what justice is (in the biblical texts wisdom is closely associated with justice).[20] Admittedly, in our present situation where the young need to be challenged to embrace the value of age there isn't always the assumption from our present youth population that 'the aged are always wise'. However, the value of this text is a challenge to older people themselves, who would seek to assert that age is preferable to youth in matters of wisdom. It is certainly an attitude that I have come across in previous churches, where my views have been dismissed purely on account of my age, which, one might add, is as much an example of age discrimination as is dismissing the views of an older person. But the writer of Job does not describe Job or his companions as interrupting Elihu's speeches. Instead an example of the humility of the older person who is willing to learn from those who are younger is presented in these verses. Perhaps it is that true wisdom in old age comes in the knowledge that one's own wisdom is insignificant to that of the sovereign God, who uses whomsoever he wills to convey his incomparable wisdom to the older person. One of the sources he

---

[19] (*continued*) the young Elihu who, because of his overly apologetic and apparently boastful manner, has 'suffered greatly in biblical interpretation'. Hartley in the same passage observes that 'Elihu's relationship with Job differs from that of the other three comforters … he is a young, promising wise man who attempts to offer some new insight into the issue of Job's suffering' (Hartley, *The Book of Job*, p. 449).

[20] Hartley, *The Book of Job*, p. 434.

may well use is the younger person. The humility of old age shown by the writer in this discourse is that Job and his companions are presented as listening, regardless of reaction once Elihu has concluded. This is a lesson that all of us need to be constantly reminded of, as it may help to identify and answer the issue of generational conflict when it occurs in the church.

Psalm 71

One commentator has described Psalm 71 as a 'psalm for old age'.[21] The psalm contains personal details of a man's life, but it is also a form of prayer by which an oppressed person can bring his or her distress and needs before God.[22] The text of the psalm reveals this distress not only in the context of the immediate situation, where the psalmist is facing danger: 'For my enemies speak against me; those who wait to kill me conspire together' (verse 10). But in old age suffering has befallen this man and to those of his own time he has become a sign of what they to could become: 'I have become a portent to many …' (verse 7). He looks not only to his present situation, but in presenting a plea for his future, which appears here to be uncertain in the face of increasing frailty, he cries out: 'Do not cast me away when I am old; do not forsake me when my strength is gone' (verse 9) and 'Even when I am old and grey, do not forsake me, O God…' (verse 18). The writer's recognition of the frailty of his age is clear, as he describes himself as on old man (verses 9, 17ff.), but so is his sense of faithful past and future, as verse 5 of the psalm declares: 'For you

---

[21] D. Kidner, *Psalms 1–72* (Inter-Varsity Press, 1973), p. 250.

[22] H.J. Kraus, *Psalms 60–150: A Continental Commentary*, Hilton C. Oswald (tr.) (Augsburg Fortress, 1989), p. 72.

have been my hope, O Sovereign Lord, my confidence since my youth.'

The theologian H.J. Kraus observes of this psalm that it:

> radiates tremendous assurance. The man who always conducted his life in the light of God's wonderful deeds and in praise of the great saving acts is even now, when his strength is diminishing in the last great threat, supported by Israel's songs of praise.[23]

The Psalm presents us again with the threat that old age brought, and reminds us that this threat was not only known by women such as Naomi in the book of Ruth, but also by men. These were older people attempting to reconcile themselves to their outward condition of increasing vulnerability, yet Psalm 71 speaks of a further area of reconciliation in the life of the older person: the need to reconcile past and present. However, the psalmist goes further, as he doesn't only reconcile past and present, but he sees a future purpose for himself and commits to set about it, concluding in verse 18 that he will: 'declare your power to the next generation, your might to all who are to come'. The psalmist provides a sense of journey throughout, revealing something of the depth of faith of the older person, which had carried him through suffering, disbelief and despair. This is not a journey purely for the benefit of the individual, but it is for the generations that are yet to become old, for they too need to hear about the goodness and power of God. And, more importantly, the psalmist does not see his age as a barrier to doing this, because he knows the message he has to speak of: not empty words to be quoted at people, but a life resonant with the experience of journeying with the living God.

---

[23] Ibid. p. 73.

Psalm 90

This psalm has been described as 'one of the most magisterial of the psalms'.[24] The theologian Walter Brueggemann suggests that psalm 90:

> be heard as though Moses were now at Pisgah ... He has come to an end. He stands at the Promised Land to which he has been headed all his life ... Now it dawns on him that he will not go there. He embraces that painful reality that his life-pursuit of fidelity will stop short of fruition. He submits to that reality from God – but that does not stop the yearning.[25]

This wondrous psalm provides us with the picture of an older man aware of the finitude of his life and considering the place he had reached, which moves him to present his final plea before God. Some have read this psalm as being principally about the numbering of days as the individual becomes aware of the temporality of life. However, this reading alone is not enough: there is more to this psalm and the concern of the older man, Moses, presented here than merely the numbering of days lived. It also contains the idea of evaluation; of considering the days and life lived.[26] Such an evaluation is not one of self-pity or regret, as the psalmist ensures with his opening verse that this evaluation is held in the light of the everlasting nature of God, who has 'been our dwelling place throughout all generations'. This is not a man who having weighed up his life finds nothing of consolation, for God is his consolation. If ever there was a psalm directed at the older person

---

[24] W. Brueggemann, *The Message of the Psalms: A Theological Commentary* (Augsburg, 1984), p. 110.

[25] Ibid. pp. 110–11.

[26] M.E. Tate, *Psalms 51–100* (Word, 1990), pp. 442–3.

at his or her life's end, this is it, as the psalmist can recognize both the affliction of life and the splendour of knowing God.

Brueggemann considers verse 12 to be the pivotal point and asserts that 'The psalm affirms that the goal of true prayer, piety, and spirituality is finally to have "a wise heart".'[27] To be taught to number our days aright so that we might gain a heart of wisdom is a lesson that only one who had lived that long life of 70 or 80 years (see verse 10) could teach. I was in a hospital recently supporting a couple who had lost their baby in the early stages of pregnancy. Both are wonderful parents and have a very real desire to be parents, but as I sat with the husband he asked the question 'Why?' Thankfully, he didn't expect an answer from me, but what I did observe was that neither of us could answer that question at our current stages of life. This sort of question can only be seen in the light of a life lived with God over many years, and even then the answer may be never found, but at least an experience of life might be known to be able to hold the question 'why' within its boundaries. I wonder how many leaders of churches work actively to encourage older people to grow in their knowledge of God through piety, prayer and spirituality? Without such growth none of us, whether 70, 80, or just 30, will be able to live with questions such as 'why' in our own lives. Moses knew days of affliction and years of trouble (see verse 15) but still he could state in verse 16: 'May your deeds be shown to your servants, your splendour to their children.' His journey of life with the everlasting God and the continual growth in relationship with God that his journey brought meant he had the experience of life with God within which to hold the question 'Why?' Further still, the older man Moses knew

---

[27] Brueggemann, *The Message of the Psalms*, p. 111.

that death could not rob him of what he had yet to see accomplished in his own lifetime. As Brueggemann observed, this was Moses standing at Pisgah, looking from the mountain across into the land he had been leading the people to all his life, and yet this was the land that he knew he himself was not going to enter. The experience of his journey of life with the everlasting God meant that Moses knew he could trust God's promises and leave in death to God that which was unfinished in his own temporal lifetime.

Ecclesiastes

Ecclesiastes 4:13 observes: 'Better a poor but wise youth than an old but foolish king who no longer knows how to take warning.' The emphasis of this verse develops the theme that old age and wisdom do not necessarily develop together as 'it is precisely the mark of a wise man to take counsel'.[28] Ecclesiastes provides a similar message to the story of Job, with its inclusion of the young Elihu, though here the message is far clearer – do not assume that age always beats youth in God's economy.

In Chapter 2 we considered the increasing power and wealth that will end up in the hands of older people, bringing with it potential conflict between generations, as societal resources are used to sustain an increasingly older population. Over coming years older Christians will have increasing opportunities to demonstrate to their peers the wisdom in taking counsel. In our individualistic society there is an increasing preference for self-sufficiency that argues people need no one but themselves and that people can be their own counsel in matters of wisdom in their

---

[28] R.E. Murphy, *Ecclesiastes* (Word, 1992), p. 42.

lives. It is no wonder that self-sufficiency is the antithesis of Christ-sufficiency, where in lives completely reliant upon God's grace in Jesus Christ we to take counsel from whomsoever God gives us, whether they be older or younger. The community of the church has much to say and show to an individualistic society through the way it conducts relationships between people of all ages. Though repeating the earlier point that age discrimination can occur in reverse if the church is not careful, I know of one able young curate who took up a post in a large Anglican church. At a meeting of some of the church congregation, where people were being introduced, this young curate explained to those present how during his training he found that participants on his course older than himself had not taken him seriously because of his age. When he was offered the post of curate at this large church some had even said that someone so 'young' should not take such a role. The purpose in sharing this previous experience had been to explain both where this curate had come from and his hopes for his newly ordained role. However, unfortunately, the next person who got up after the curate expressed interest in what had been said, but doubted the validity of his experience, because he was too young to understand such matters ... Truly it is better to be a poor youth than an old and foolish king!

The Old Testament clearly portrays the negative attributes of ageing with its frailty and fear and in Ecclesiastes 12:1–7, mentioned in the opening of this chapter, the writer observes the way in which old age leads to death. There is a clear realism to these verses, setting out the reality of the end of life. Death truly is the one thing that we can be certain of in this life. However, how are we prepared for death?

One interpretation of the prevalence of fear in older age is the individual's increasing realization of the finitude of his or her life, and many who do not know the salvation of Jesus Christ face that fear depending on 'internal' rather than 'eternal' resources. Older members of our churches need to be enabled to develop and grow in their understanding and use of 'eternal' resources. Rhena Taylor in her recent book *Three Score Years – and Then?* observes from her own work that she tries to keep in mind a comment made by an older woman who had been a church member all her life:

> She spoke [of] her need for the church to help her re-adjust to her changing position in the community of the church, and to make sense of her ageing in the light of her faith. It was not that she felt her church were uncaring, nor that she was not loved there, but at this time of need, she felt that their attention was elsewhere.[29]

Taylor's comment that the church's attention was 'elsewhere' at this vital time in a woman's life is a powerful observation. When she needed help to negotiate the realities of ageing in the light of her faith, the church was taken up with other matters, and failed this older woman.

The stark reality of Ecclesiastes 12:1–7 and its observations of old age makes me sit up each time I read it as I realize the journey that I have still ahead of me, no matter what advances medical science may come up with to keep me going. The power of such a piece of Scripture that moves us to consider our own ageing is tremendous and our responsibility not to then leave it at the level of intellectual engagement is great. For in leaving it at the level of the mind we fail to engage with our own fears of ageing in order to submit them before God. The danger of not doing this is that in order to forget what is ahead we

---

[29] R. Taylor, *Three Score Years – and Then?* (Monarch, 2001), p. 16.

give our attention to what is 'elsewhere' and in doing so deny older people in our midst the opportunity to be supported in their journey through the uncertainty of older age. What an incredible indictment it is for any church – that an older person who has journeyed long and hard with Christ finds him or herself forgotten because his or her journey now represents that which others would prefer to forget in their own lives. Such a situation is ironic, as an older member of the church in his or her journey through older age could be a resource and role model to future generations still to experience old age. In this failure to support not only does the older person lose out – so do the future generations.

Proverbs 16:31 and 20:29

These two proverbs when read together provide an image of the way in which old and young are inextricably linked in God's plan for his people's journey of ageing. The first proverb, 'Grey hair is a crown of splendour; it is attained by a righteous life', returns us to the theme in Israelite culture that to have reached old age implied wisdom and virtue, since long life was considered a blessing from God.[30] The second proverb, 'The glory of young men is their strength, grey hair is the splendour of the old', reminds us again of the virtue implied by age. However, the splendour of age is contrasted with the strength of youth. The theologian Roland E. Murphy observes that: 'While the strength of a youth is not to be disdained, he has a future to face, and it is there that a true judgement of a person lies.'[31]

---

[30] R.E. Murphy, *Proverbs* (Thomas Nelson, 1988), p. 124.
[31] Ibid. p. 154.

The future to be faced and lived is one that for the young person will hopefully lead to an old age. But this was not given as a guarantee in Israelite culture, due to the physical effort of merely living. Although younger people today may not face the same hardships as the first hearers of these proverbs, they do face risks in how they live their lives. With what their bodies have to endure, the lifestyles they have can lead to an early death – to the crown of grey hair not being attained. Strength is needed to live life, strength to say no, to make choices for good, and to be prepared to stand against the prevailing culture. However, as has already been observed, the crown of grey hair is no longer celebrated, but more often derided. It is no wonder the young person lives for the moment of youth if old age is not respected in our society.

Perhaps the message of these proverbs is twofold: first, to the church, to recover the splendour of grey hair; second, to the older person, to dare to stand up and give thanks for life attained. A wonderful example of this happened during an evening service in our present church when Graham, an older and longstanding member of the church, stood up and said he wanted to offer an encouragement to everyone there about continuing in faith. He had come to know Jesus Christ as his Saviour 50 years before and here he was 50 years later, now in his mid-70s, still standing and able to witness to God's goodness and faithfulness in sustaining him throughout his life. And yes, Graham definitely wears the grey-haired 'crown of splendour'! It was a tremendous encouragement to all the younger people in the congregation, in which I include myself, to keep going, to keep on living and desiring a life that radiates with God's righteousness. Unless older people are enabled to celebrate age and younger people to receive the encouragement of this celebration, the crown of splendour and all that it signifies will be lost.

Isaiah 46:4

In the midst of the turmoil the people of Israel faced, God, through the prophet Isaiah, gives a wonderful assurance to the house of Jacob and to all who remained in Israel: 'Even to your old age and grey hairs I am he, I am he who will sustain you. I have made you and I will carry you; I will sustain you and I will rescue you.' What a promise this is! Spoken to those who had been either born in exile in Babylon or who had remained in the land during the exile, the assurance is that despite all that had happened God was still carrying his people, he was still sustaining them despite their rebelliousness and separation from the land.[32] God transcends the processes of history! In his commentary on Isaiah chapters 40–66 John N. Oswalt examines this passage and observes:

> There will never come a time when we outgrow our depend-ence on God. We are as dependent on God in old age as we were when we were infants ... Nor will there ever be a time when a doddering old grandfather-God will somehow need to lean on us, and we will need to find a young, virile god for a new age. He is not subject to history; in every age he is the unchanging *I am he*.[33]

For each generation the assurance remains the same: 'I am he who will sustain you.' What value this promise from

---

[32] A. Motyer, *Isaiah* (Inter-Varsity Press, 1999), p. 294.
[33] J.N. Oswalt, *The Book of Isaiah: Chapters 40 – 66* (Eerdmans, 1998), p. 230.

Scripture has to hold on to in older age. The promise of God, which Graham described in the previous section, to sustain us throughout our lives is one to treasure in our hearts and meditate upon. He will never grow weary or weak or tired of hearing our cries or our doubts. He is the God not only of old age but of all age, as he transcends any earthly barriers or categories.

Joel

The prophet Joel's prophecy, echoed by Peter in Acts 2, both provides us with a helpful link between the Old and New Testaments and points to the promise of the Spirit to come. Joel 2:28–32 speaks of roles for both young and old in the day of the Lord: old men will dream dreams and young men will see visions. It is a wonderful picture of how distinctions of age, sex and social class were to be removed through this common spiritual endowment[34] witnessed at the foundation of the church. In the Old Testament the majority of references to the Spirit of God are in relation to his empowering of certain individuals for particular tasks, though one example of a large-scale empowering by the Spirit of God would be the 70 elders upon whom the Spirit came in Numbers 11.[35] However, in this prophecy in Joel God is speaking of not only empowering the elder but all people, and there will be no discrimination, as far as the activity of the Spirit is concerned, in terms of age, sex or status.[36]

---

[34] L.C. Allen, *The Books of Joel, Obadiah, Jonah and Micah* (Eerdmans, 1976), p. 99.

[35] D. Prior, *The Message of Joel, Micah and Habakkuk* (Inter-Varsity Press, 1998), p. 71.

[36] Ibid. p. 73.

When reflecting upon verse 28 I have always been struck by the difference in experience for young and old: the old men will dream dreams while the young men will see visions. The use of language in this verse recognizes the experience of age. The young, through their lack of life experience, are dependent upon the provision of vision for what will be, whereas the old, with lives full of experience, both positive and negative, have a wealth from which to draw upon in their dreams. It is a subtle distinction, but an important one, if we are to see the value of all ages within the church being able to contribute to its life, while at the same time retaining generational distinctiveness of experience. To achieve this we need to be encouraging not only young people in their desiring the use of spiritual gifts in their lives, but also older people. Our pioneers are witnesses not only to their own generation but also to their children and their children's children of the goodness of the God, who journeys through life with his people bringing them to the promise of his eternal kingdom, where in Christ death has been defeated – there is no more fear.

4

Ageing in the New Testament

As we move into the New Testament in our examination of the role and value of the older person in Scripture, it is helpful to remind ourselves of what it meant to be 'aged' in this period, in which we see the increasing influence of the Greco-Roman world upon Christianity as it emerged from its Judaic roots. It is difficult to offer definitive statements about the role of the older person in antiquity, or about how old age was perceived, as many of the sources available can give quite subjective opinions influenced by personal impressions as well as political, social or economic motivations.[1] There are no fundamental biological reasons why any body in antiquity should age faster than a body would today; indeed, there is no evidence of this. What can be seen are the effects of poor diet and health, which speeded up the appearance of age, and it is this 'appearance' that catches the interest of writers.[2]

Stobaeus's collection of 95 passages from 42 different genres was mentioned in the opening of the previous chapter. In the collection are examples of the subjective

---

[1] T. Parkin, 'Ageing in Antiquity: Status and Participation' in P. Johnson and P. Thane (eds), *Old Age from Antiquity to Postmodernity* (Routledge, 1998), p. 20.

[2] Ibid. p. 22.

perceptions of writers struggling to deal with the issue of old age in society. Around the end of the first century AD a pamphlet was produced by Plutarch, entitled 'On Whether an Old Man Should Engage in Public Affairs', written when Plutarch himself was an old man.[3] He writes: 'Old age, a time of honour, provides the statesman with qualities such as reason, judgement, frankness, soundness of mind and practical wisdom ...' Plutarch concludes that if nothing else the older man should instruct the young in order to prepare them for the more prestigious positions, which were the realm of the elder statesman.[4] For Plutarch (*c.* AD 46–*c.* AD 120), as well as Seneca (*c.* 4 BC–AD 65) and Cicero (106 BC–43 BC), and many other males of the late Roman Republic or early Roman Empire, the aim was a healthy old age and the pursuing of worthwhile and rewarding activities, which, as Plutarch observed, included service to the state.[5] However, the historian and gerontologist Tim Parkin has observed that while engaging in such activity was seen as a great contribution it was also seen as a refuge from old age. Remember, it was Seneca who considered it better to leap from a crumbling building than face the vagaries of old age, which included the threat of poor physical and mental health.[6] While respect for older people tends to be typical of most societies, it has been suggested from the work of anthropologists that there is a tendency for this respect to be eroded by rising living standards, literacy and social mobility. R. Alistair Campbell in his excellent

---

[3] Ibid. p. 26.

[4] Ibid. The quotation cites Parkin's paraphrasing.

[5] Ibid. p. 29.

[6] Ibid. See p. 28 for Parkin's lengthy and useful quote of Seneca, considered one of the most heartfelt and careful statements from antiquity about the realities faced in old age.

book *The Elders*, which looks at seniority in earliest Christianity, observes that in the light of such factors contributing to the erosion of respect 'We would ... expect to find within the ancient world a high respect for the old, but also a tendency for this to be challenged by increased urbanization.'[7] Therefore, considering available sources from the ancient world, what we see is an erosion of respect occurring as writers struggled with not only the existence and presence of old age but with the realities of the old age they themselves faced.

The pressure of an ageing population, which we are currently experiencing, is not found in antiquity.[8] Older people formed a low proportion of the population and this remained a relatively unchanging demographic situation in Greek and Roman history. Neither was the issue of 'old age' a pressure faced by the early church in the immediacy of its institution. However, it was to become an issue in the church's provision of social welfare and the need to disciple steadily ageing congregations, as people who had become Christians grew older.

Age in the New Testament finds itself expressed in much the same way as in the Old Testament. Christianity

---

[7] R. Alistair Campbell, *The Elders: Seniority in Earliest Christianity* (T&T Clark, 1994), p. 240.

[8] M.I. Finley, 'The Elderly in Classical Antiquity' in T.M. Faulkner and J. De Luce, *Old Age in Greek and Latin Literature* (State of New York University Press, 1989). In the introductory chapter Finley notes that there were points of demographic fluctuation in time and place, probably due to socio-economic factors and other contingent factors. See also D.I. Kertzer and P. Laslett, *Aging in the Past: Demography, Society and Old Age* (University of California Press, 1995). Here they draw attention to Ulpian's life table from third century AD as a pre-statistical example of population and age. Though not reliable for demographers, it does demonstrate existence of older populations and their proportion.

continues the principle of care for the widow, for the poor and the oppressed. There continues a fundamental respect for older people and, as we shall see, this included a role in leadership. The differences begin to occur when one considers the world that surrounded the early church in which the respect once given to age was being challenged to the point where Christianity was to become a distinctive voice through its care, respect and provision for older people.

During this chapter the intention is to follow much the same order as Chapter 3, using broad brushstrokes to highlight some key aspects from the Gospel accounts, as well as the writings of Paul and others. No doubt there will be aspects missed or not explained as fully as they could, be but once again my hope is that what follows may serve as a stimulus to thought, response and application.

Elizabeth and Zechariah

The Gospel of Luke opens with a series of depictions of older role models. The first example is the elderly couple Elizabeth and Zechariah (Luke 1:5–25, 39–45, 57–80), who were to become the parents of John the Baptist. The story bears similarities to that of Abraham and Sarah – both stories contain events that were initiated by the action of God. However, similarities end, as the birth of John in Luke's Gospel runs in direct parallel to that of the birth of Jesus.[9] Elizabeth, a married woman advanced in years and therefore unable to conceive, becomes pregnant and recognizes the way in which her God has removed from her the social disgrace of childlessness and in doing so has shown her favour. Elizabeth is to be the first to declare the

---

[9] I.H. Marshall, *The Gospel of Luke* (Paternoster Press, 1998), p. 49.

Lordship of Jesus when, upon meeting the pregnant Mary, she proclaims (verse 43): 'But why am I so favoured, that the mother of my Lord should come to me?' It is the elderly Zechariah, having had his mouth opened again after the Lord had closed it because of his lack of belief, who is then filled with the Holy Spirit and prophesies about the unborn child Jesus, looking forward to the promised Messiah and the redemption of Israel. Zechariah's prophecy continues and from verse 76 it focuses on the role God had purposed for Zechariah and Elizabeth's son, John, as the one who would prepare the way for the Lord. From the very start of his Gospel account Luke includes older people interacting with the young Mary and acting as witnesses to the coming Messiah – Jesus.

Simeon

After the birth of Jesus Luke's narrative continues with the presentation of the young Jesus at the Temple (2:21ff.) and once again it is an older person who recognizes the person of Christ. Luke records the figures of Simeon and Anna, two people of old age. The meeting of Simeon with the baby Messiah is an encounter he had been anticipating for many years (Luke 2:25–35). Theologian I. Howard Marshall observes that although Simeon is not explicitly referred to as being of 'old age' he should be considered elderly due to Luke's reference to his many years of waiting and his expectation of death.[10] In his encounter with Jesus in the precincts of the Temple Simeon recognizes the fulfilment of God's purposes and promises in his life as he sees the Messiah and holds him in his arms.

---

[10] Ibid. p. 119.

Simeon, upon whom was the Holy Spirit (verse 25), must have been an extraordinary person to know. Consider the patience with which he had lived, waiting all his life for this moment. I always find it an encouragement to meet an older person who has known Christ for a long time, whose life radiates with Jesus at every point, not in a way that is brash or obvious, but with an understated humility that leaves you knowing deep inside that you have just met someone who truly knows the Lord.

Every so often I visit a member of our congregation called Michael, who is 91. He is an older man whose life radiates with Christ – though I doubt he would ever agree with that observation! His life hasn't been easy and recently he lost his wife after 64 years of marriage. But one of the joys of visiting Michael is that it is wonderful to sit and simply 'be' with him, to hear him talk of the way God helped him out of bed one morning when his knees wouldn't work, or the time he asked God to remind him how to tie a tie. Each instance reflects an aspect of life many would take for granted, but for Michael, now well into his fourth age, this is simply how he lives his days: with Jesus. It is tremendously encouraging to spend time with someone whose life is about a constant conversation with God and I firmly believe that such a level of relationship with the Lord only comes from a lifetime of patiently waiting upon him.

In Luke 2 Simeon takes the young Jesus into his arms, and the words he speaks have been recorded in church tradition, expressed in the words of the *Nunc Dimittis* (Song of Simeon). The aged Simeon realizes the fulfilment of God's past promises in the present moment and, as Howard Marshall observes, he can now entrust himself to death, which is his future, knowing that life and immortality have been brought to light. 'He [Simeon] believes that God's word has been fulfilled without any outward sign, save that he saw a child at the time and place stated by God.'[11] I must admit a personal frustration as an Anglican minister. The *Nunc Dimittis* finds its primary expression in the liturgy of Evening Prayer in the Anglican Church; its context in Anglican liturgy is the close of a day. The response of the congregation is: 'Save us, O Lord, while waking, and guard us while sleeping, that awake we may watch with Christ and asleep may rest in peace.'[12] I express this frustration not because I don't like the *Nunc Dimittis*, or because I have some problem with the use of liturgy, but because Simeon's song is a most wonderful declaration of old age, a telling of faithfulness lived and witnessed in the life of the older person. Simeon's statement of being dismissed in peace is one of being able to face death in old age not with fear but with the joy of promise fulfilled. It is not about the close of a single day but the close of a life. For this reason I've appreciated being able to make use of Simeon's song in the Church of England's recently introduced Common Worship Funeral Liturgy. However, there remains a great spiritual depth to be explored in this statement, made by an older person. It could be a great challenge and encouragement. But perhaps it must first be recovered and used at points outside of a liturgical structure in order for its full expression of the joy of promise fulfilled in a person's life to be visible.

Anna

Immediately after the encounter with Simeon recorded in Luke's Gospel we come to the meeting of Anna with the young Jesus in the Temple precincts (Luke 2:36–8). Luke

---

[11] Ibid. p. 120.
[12] Quoted from *Common Worship* (Church House, 2000).

makes particular note of Anna's age, her marriage and then subsequent widowhood, her continuous worship in the Temple and her being a prophetess. This is of considerable importance as the portrayal of elderly women in antiquity was often negative. Extending outside of the New Testament period, the early church saw a number of older women acting as powerful witnesses – older women supported a number of the early church Fathers. The canonical order of widows – women who embraced widowhood, who remained virtuous and did not remarry – was regarded in the church as a great witness to Christ. However, here in Scripture we see an elderly woman fulfilling a vital role of witness. Like Simeon's encounter this is a story resonant with meaning for the spiritual life of the older person.

J. Gordon Harris makes an important observation regarding this encounter of Anna's, noting 'Her old age does not keep her from becoming an early witness of the Messiah.' [13] This is a vital statement to grasp, for I wonder how many older women are precluded from being witnesses of Jesus simply on the basis of age, or the cultural stereotyping of what an older woman can or can't do? What do older women in the church get offered first: the tea and coffee rota or helping on an Alpha course? Before I get myself into trouble, I think doing the tea and coffee rota is an admirable job, but what needs to be challenged is what an older woman might be asked by others to do *first* in a church setting. Admittedly, there is the issue of whether or not she would be comfortable helping on, for example, an Alpha course. But this isn't about what people *volunteer* to do, rather it is about what they are *asked* to do in the life of the church – the two are very different. Reticence

---

[13] J. Gordon Harris, *God and the Elderly* (Fortress Press, 1987), pp. 79–80.

on the part of the older woman has more to do with having spent a lifetime being prepared for a narrow church stereotype of what older women 'should' do instead of being encouraged to break out of past moulds and receive the tremendous scriptural heritage of older women in God's plan. As I'm writing I am reminded of a number of older women in our own church, though some will not appreciate the 'older' tag! Rosemary and Jackie have served as missionaries overseas for much of their lives and Margaret continues to do so even now. Thelma has been a part of the church for years and has impacted the lives of many there and Issy has just retired from a successful career and has done everything from being a very busy churchwarden to the coffee rota! Joan served in a religious order for a number of years, has just started to lead retreats and serves on a visiting team to housebound people. Jill has a wonderful ministry amongst international students, as does Marjorie. These are names that won't mean a great deal written here on the page, but this is a small selection of older women who have been, and will continue to be, witnesses to Jesus. All of these women I sincerely hope will never be precluded from being a witness to Christ merely on the arbitrary basis of age and will be willing to break out of any pre-set mould any church might try and fit them into!

Simeon and Anna

Before moving on, there is one final aspect that must be recognized about Simeon and Anna: simply the extraordinary truth that Luke uses older people as witnesses at the beginning of his Gospel. Perhaps Luke was building a powerful foundation of testimony, establishing the credibility of his witnesses. Who better than this series of older people, especially Simeon and Anna, who are prophetic

figures, both aged, pious, related to the Temple and awaiting the promised Messiah, and who both recognize in
Jesus God's redemptive intervention in the world.[14] There is
something of the dignity of old age that is expressed in these
stories of lives lived with God. Simeon and Anna's fullness
of passion for him gives them integrity as witnesses.[15]

Gordon Harris observes of the Simeon and Anna
encounters that 'These positive images of older people
show that the Synoptic Gospels do not demean old age
when they reject the doctrines of ancient tradition.'[16]
Whether one agrees with Gordon Harris or not about
Simeon and Anna rejecting ancient doctrines (by this he is
referring to Judaism), or whether they were viewing their
fulfilment in their recognition of Jesus as God's promised
Messiah, what these passages do observe are two older
people as messengers and witnesses to change. Here was
the kingdom of God breaking into the world in the form
of child, and it was to be the older women and men –
Elizabeth, Zechariah, Simeon and Anna – who were to be
key figures in recognizing the coming kingdom.

The Widow's Example

In chapter 21 of his Gospel Luke presents us with the
widow who is praised by Jesus for giving the last of her
money to the Temple in Jerusalem.[17] This woman is held

[14] J.B. Green, *The Gospel of Luke* (Eerdmans, 1997), p. 150.

[15] J. Nolland, *Luke 1 – 9:20* (Word, 1989), p. 125.

[16] Harris, *God and the Elderly*, pp. 79–80.

[17] This story comes at the start of the chapter, which precedes
the Lukan passion narrative. It also occupies a similar point in
Mark chapter 12, also preceding the passion narrative. In
both cases this story is only separated by the account of the

up as an example of virtue rather than as a consumer of other people's virtue. It is this contrast between what is true and false piety that Luke offers in this passage (also contained in Mark). I. Howard Marshall comments on this passage: 'The incident fits in with Luke's emphasis on the way in which true religion affects a person's attitude to wealth … the widow gave all that she had and thereby expressed her faith in God to provide for her needs.'[18] Luke's account also serves as a reminder of the precarious position of the widow, in contrast to Anna, who is portrayed as someone commanding respect. Here the widow gives all that she has – there is nothing more. Poverty in the first-century context is best understood as absolute rather than our more modern 'relative' developed-world understanding. J.J. Meggitt in his book on the subject of poverty in the first century, *Paul, Poverty and Survival*, offers the following definition: 'The poor are those living at or near subsistence level, whose prime concern it is to obtain the minimum food, shelter, and clothing necessary to sustain life, whose lives are dominated by the struggle for physical survival.'[19] As part of the developed world we do not always see the same level of absolute poverty as the norm for a significant proportion of our population. But we come very close at times with our elderly population, particularly when we read newspaper stories each year about older people who die because they cannot afford to heat their own homes.

---

[17] (*continued*) signs of the end of the age. Therefore, one would suggest that it is of note that the example of the widow's offering is to be found at such a significant point.

[18] Marshall, *The Gospel of Luke*, p. 750.

[19] J.J. Meggitt, *Paul, Poverty and Survival* (T. & T. Clark, 1998), p. 5. Meggitt's definition of the poor is a quote from Peter Garney.

However, in many of our churches, how often do we miss the contribution of the less-wealthy older person in the midst of other still economically active (and therefore younger) people? Michael Apichella has titled his recent book on empowering the older generation *The Church's Hidden Asset*.[20] Like the widow in Luke's Gospel, older people can be hidden amongst the more prominent and 'in vogue' assets. Apichella observes of this story and the widow involved:

> where does one find the faith to act in this way? I believe that her faith grew over many years of trusting God to meet her needs – physical, mental and emotional. What's more, I believe that her faith was the result of a deep conviction that the Lord would not allow her charity to cause her to starve. To give away all that one has for God's sake is the act of a person who has had a long and nourishing relationship with God, a relationship that had been growing over many years.[21]

Were it not for Jesus pointing out to his disciples the example of this woman, she would have remained a 'hidden asset'. But with her story in the open she is an asset to the ever-advancing kingdom of God. Our churches are full of such hidden assets, waiting for someone to recognize them and show how they witness to God's faithfulness and goodness that endures forever.

---

[20] M. Apichella, *The Church's Hidden Asset: Empowering the Older Generation* (Kevin Mayhew, 2001).

[21] Ibid. pp. 33–4.

Care for the Older Person

Luke's Gospel continues as a rich source of examples of older people through his concern that true religion would impact the life and action of the Christian. One example is Jesus' recorded denunciation of those who abuse positions of trust, consuming widows' houses (Luke 20:47), most likely referring to those who were appointed as the guardians of property after the death of a husband.[22] There is a similar event in Mark's Gospel, where Jesus chastised the Pharisees and Scribes for using the religious vow of Corban (an offering to God) as an excuse not to support elderly parents.[23] These passages, combined with that about the widow whose only son had died (Luke 7:11–16) and so faced severe hardship, contain a concern for the welfare of older people that would overflow into the early church's concern to provide care for people. However, Luke 7:12 is particularly interesting, as the text reads in the NIV that: 'As he approached the town gate, a dead person was being carried out – the only son of his mother, and she was a widow …' It is as though Luke, by highlighting the woman's circumstance as a widow, is suggesting that the impact of her son's death was all the greater, not because she was his mother, but because his death left her alone as a widow.

Jesus demonstrates in these passages not only a concern to care for older people but also a willingness to uncover

---

[22] See Marshall, *The Gospel of Luke*, p. 750 for a discussion of how various scholars have interpreted who those in positions of trust might have been.

[23] Harris, *God and the Elderly*, p. 81. Harris provides a helpful discussion of Mark 7:1–13, setting in context the common failure to apply 'law' as it had been intended for the benefit of the suffering individual.

injustice. In Chapter 1 of this book the issue of elder abuse and the injustices older people receive at the hands of others was briefly outlined. A personal concern is the lack of training and awareness within national churches around this issue. The failure of any church adequately to protect vulnerable older people does seem to fly in the face of Christ's concern for the older person facing abuse by those who have been charged with his or her care.

Jesus' Example

Some have suggested that Jesus' own concern for his family, particularly his mother, was lacking. They point to Matthew 12:46–50, where Jesus is told his mother and brothers are looking for him, and he replies by asking who his mother and brothers are, declaring those who do God's will to be his brother, sister and mother.[24] R.T. France has observed that Jesus' words have been taken to imply a lack of proper respect for his mother.[25] However, the emphasis of this passage is not the disowning of family, rather that 'there is a tie which is closer even than that of family'.[26] It would appear highly spurious to describe as hypocritical Jesus' teaching regarding older people based on some notion that Matthew 12 represents a dismissal of family. Rather, the chapter demonstrates the orientation of relationship between God and person. This does not exclude the notion of family. As we have already seen, Jesus shows a clear concern towards the older person, and personally I find the words of Jesus recorded at his crucifixion in John's Gospel to be an

---

[24] See also parallel passages in Mark 3:31 and Luke 8:19–21.

[25] R.T. France, *Matthew* (IVP, 1985), p. 215.

[26] Ibid.

amazing statement of care for an older person – his mother, Mary (John 19:26–7):

> When Jesus saw his mother there, and the disciple whom he loved standing near by, he said to his mother, 'Dear woman, here is your son,' and to the disciple, 'Here is your mother.' From that time on, this disciple took her into his home.

Don Carson has observed that while brothers and sisters existed who would have cared for Mary they are absent from the crucifixion scene. Therefore it is Jesus' prerogative as the first-born son to hand the care of his mother to the disciple John.[27] It is astonishing that at such a point of pain and certainty of death care is demonstrated. The provision for the older person – Jesus' mother – is key.

It is reasonable to observe from the Gospel accounts that there is no clearly specific teaching regarding the care of the older person. However, it is possible to see a thread of compassion and inspired care running through the life and teaching of Jesus, often recorded in the contexts of other stories. Thus compassion can be seen up to the point of his death, and beyond, in the inspired teaching of leaders of the church such as James, Jesus' brother.

James

This Christ-inspired compassion finds expression in the following saying of James: 'Religion that God our Father accepts as pure and faultless is this: to look after orphans and widows in their distress and to keep oneself from

---

[27] D. Carson, *The Gospel According to John* (IVP, 1994). See pp. 616–18 for a brief discussion of the themes raised in this passage (John 19:26–7).

being polluted by the world' (James 1:27). Here James uses the word 'religion' positively and in a sense we are increasingly losing, giving it both practical content and outworking.[28] This is not meant as a comprehensive definition of Christianity, but it does point to the way in which lives should be lived,[29] including care for the vulnerable older woman, the widow. William Booth, founder of the Salvation Army, ensuring both a practical content and outworking, said: 'We will wash it [our money] in the tears of the widows and orphans and lay it on the altar of humanity.'[30] As we have seen in this and the previous chapter, care is not to be reserved for the point of distress or crisis. Care is to run through the life of the older person and beyond, as seen in the concern of Ruth and the instruction of Jesus on the cross to his disciple. This 'care' is both a divine instruction to the individual to care for the older person and also a challenge to the older person to be an inspirer of care.

Ralph Martin, in his commentary on James, gives a helpful insight into this verse, drawing out the application of the word 'religion':

> it stands for the outward expression of faith in liturgy and worship, and so it reminds us that however inward looking and individualistic personal trust must be there is also a horizontal plane on which true faith operates. Faith unites us to God in Christ; it also relates us to our fellow men and women.[31]

We cannot decline our responsibility to one another in Christ. Old or young, we are all related to one another, and

---

[28] R.P. Martin, *James* (Word, 1988), p. 54.
[29] J. Adamson, *The Epistle of James* (Eerdmans, 1976), p. 85.
[30] William Booth quoted in ibid. p. 86.
[31] Martin, *James*, p. 54.

there is a need to care for each other, to recognize one another in the context of the body of Christ, and to rejoice that in Christ we are united in the glorious promise of eternal life with him. One of the most enjoyable evening services I have been to in the last year was when the service leader encouraged the young people in the service to go and say thank you to and pray with an older member of the church. It was enjoyable because I watched as people united in Christ and related to one another looked beyond the outward appearances of age and rejoiced in God with one another.

Paul's View of Old Age

The issue of old age appears in Paul's teachings, though it is mainly dealt with as a matter of concern in the Pastoral Epistles. There is little mention of the issue of old age made elsewhere in Paul's letters.[32] J. Gordon Harris makes the

---

[32] Harris, *God and the Elderly*, p. 84 comments that Paul seems unconcerned by the issue of intergenerational conflict. Pointing to Galatians 3:28–9 Harris argues that this is an omission from Paul's list of societal divisions. However, Harris fails to grasp the 'all-encompassing' nature of Paul's list. Were he to have listed every division found within society it would certainly have taken more than a couple of verses! One could argue that Paul has left out the division of rich and poor, the division of ethnicity, the division of colour, and so on. Each of these are 'inferred' in Galatians 3:28–9, which is not intended as a defining list of societal division. Rather it is an example of the use of rhetoric applied by Paul in defending the new-found freedom in Christ. Paul's lack of inclusion of teaching regarding the aged in his earlier writing may also have an eschatological context. Some scholars have suggested that during the time in which Paul's early letters were written, the imminent

helpful observation that the inclusion of references to old age, or rather older people, is due to a now ageing church leadership and membership. This ageing church leadership required more support as it came under pressure from certain younger members.[33]

The opening verses of 1 Timothy 5 contain a number of references to the role of older people and attitudes towards them in the early church: 'Do not rebuke an older man harshly, but exhort him as if he were your father. Treat ... older women as mothers ... ' (5:1–2). Here Paul is simply telling Timothy as a younger leader not to rebuke older members of the church by browbeating them with the power and force of an argument. Rather, Paul instructs Timothy to encourage them, to use gentle persuasion, and in doing so treat older members with respect, dignity and honour.[34] William D. Mounce observes that in the context of Paul's letter this instruction is clearly related to Paul's household view of the church, seen in 1 Timothy 3:15: 'you will know how people are to conduct themselves in God's household, which is the church of the living God, the pillar and foundation of the truth'.[35] However, Paul was not inferring that Timothy, as a younger leader, was to become a doormat, only ever displaying a 'welcome' sign to whatever an older person wanted to do in the church. Instead, Paul's concern is about how Timothy leads: it is

---

[32] (*continued*) second coming was still expected. Therefore Paul's primary concern would not have been teaching regarding the role of older people in congregations.

[33] Harris, *God and the Elderly*, p. 87 also notes that the increasing incidence of teachings about widows and other elders to found in these epistles gives an indication of the increasing needs of an ageing population within the early church.

[34] W.D. Mounce, *Pastoral Epistles* (Word, 2000), pp. 268–70.

[35] Ibid.

his approach to leadership that will or will not win the respect of older people: 'Don't let anyone look down on you because you are young, but set an example for the believers in speech, in life, in love, in faith and in purity' (1 Timothy 4:12). If ever a younger leader needed an example of what to do and say, this is it, and it is pretty basic stuff! Displaying Christ-likeness and not being enamoured by the world's idea of leadership that strips another person of his or her power by force – this is what marks out the Christian leader as being distinctive. It is this same message that Peter repeated in his first letter: 'Young men, in the same way be submissive to those who are older. All of you, clothe yourselves with humility toward one another, because, "God opposes the proud but gives grace to the humble"' (1 Peter 5:5).

There was an important purpose in giving instruction to younger leaders in how to teach and lead older members of the church. In a missionary church, which had experienced rapid expansion particularly through Paul's mission to the Gentiles, the situation was one that had led to the conversion of older people. Paul's letter to Titus concerns Titus's work on Crete amongst new converts, including older people. Paul's concern for older women not to drink too much is a fascinating observation in the light of older women's common portrayal as alcoholics. But Paul's concern was not just about behaviour: it was also that these older women, though new converts, had a role in being reverent in the way they lived, as by their examples they were also teachers to those around them of 'what is good' (2:3). Similarly, older men were to be faithful witnesses of Christ through their lives. It is interesting to note the words Paul uses in his instruction to Titus: that he should teach these older men to be self-controlled, sound in faith, in love and in endurance (2:2).

These are all familiar terms that Paul used of his own relationship with Christ.

The fourth-century church leader John Chrysostom also pays attention to Paul's instructions to the younger leader, Timothy, particularly those of 1 Timothy 5:1. When Paul writes 'Do not rebuke an elder' Chrysostom asks 'Is he now speaking of the order? I think not, but of any elderly man.' And again, Chrysostom observes: 'Rebuke is in its own nature offensive, particularly when it is addressed to an old man, and when it proceeds from a young man ...'[36] Regarding the requirement in 1 Timothy 5:19 of two or more witnesses to bring a charge against an elder, Chrysostom states: 'For he speaks of an elder not with respect to office, but to age, since the young more easily fall into sin than their elders ...'[37] While it is more than possible for an older person to lack virtue, Chrysostom still insists on the need to respect those in old age. This is not to suggest Chrysostom was advocating a state whereby people in old age could not be corrected and called to account for their actions. Chrysostom repeats Paul's instruction to Timothy, insisting that respect for age is to be retained: 'What then if he should need correction? Do not rebuke him, but address him as you would a father offending.'[38]

When one considers Paul's instructions to Timothy one must hold in mind Paul's own concerns about

---

[36] *Nicene and Post-Nicene Fathers*, available online at < www.ccel. org/fathers2/ >. See John Chrysostom, Vol. 13, *Homilies on the Epistles to the Galatians, Ephesians, Philippians, Colossians, Thessalonians, Timothy, Titus, and Philemon: Homilies on the First Epistle of St Paul to Timothy*, Homily 13.

[37] Vol. 13, *Homilies on the Epistles to the Galatians, Ephesians, Philippians, Colossians, Thessalonians, Timothy, Titus, and Philemon: Homilies on the First Epistle of St Paul to Timothy*, Homily 15.

[38] Ibid.

leadership; about power and strength. Paul was the man who learnt that Christ's grace was sufficient for him and in doing so discovered power in weakness, an attitude that marks his letters with his compassion for people and passion for Jesus. However, Paul did not keep the lessons he had learnt as a leader to himself. Paul and Timothy were in relationship, the older man, Paul, encouraging and mentoring the younger man, Timothy. Theirs is not the only example. 1 Peter 5:13 records Peter's similarly supportive relationship with the younger Mark. In his commentary on 1 Peter, Peter H. Davids describes the relationship seen between Peter and Mark, observing that: 'we have a loving relationship between an older Christian and a younger, perhaps in terms of teacher-disciple ... but at least in terms of senior-respectful junior'.[39] I know a number of people who are leaders in the church who have benefited from such relationships and I would include my wife and myself in that count. How wonderful it would be to extend such relationships out into the church at large, developing mentoring whereby older people can support younger people at all stages of their lives. One small example of this was at a church I attended where there was a wonderful policy of older members of the church 'sponsoring' a family through the process of the baptism of a child. It meant not only a point of contact with the church, which was followed through and developed over time, but it also blessed that family with someone who could be a support in prayer and counsel. Such a practical outworking of relationships between older and younger people in the church is something that we don't celebrate very well. It seems to pass by without anyone really noticing. It would be marvellous to hear more of the older and younger

---

[39]   P.H. Davids, *The First Epistle of Peter* (Eerdmans, 1990), p. 204.

person speaking about what a relationship/friendship in Christ had brought into their lives.

As one would expect, Paul continues the theme of teaching regarding vulnerable older women who were widows, found in the Old Testament and in the teachings of Jesus. He writes to Timothy (1 Timothy 5:1–16, NRSV):

> Honour widows who are really widows. If a widow has children or grandchildren, they should first learn their religious duty to their own family and make some repayments to their parents; for this is pleasing in God's sight … Let a widow be put on the list if she is not less than sixty years old and has been married only once.[40]

The reference to widows is of significance, not only because it mentions the age of 60, after which the widow is placed upon the list for support,[41] but also because of the further discussion that takes place about not including younger widows within such a list. Younger widows were seen as more able to support, or find support, for themselves. Older widows, those over 60, were seen as vulnerable and in need of the support of the church, and so once again this passage confirms the reality of the vulnerability older women faced.

This is a difficult passage as it states issues of respect and support to be expected in old age and a responsibility to care. If the elderly person has children or grandchildren they are to offer 'payment', or rather 'repayment', for the

---

[40] See Gordon Harris's discussion of this passage in *God and the Elderly*, pp. 87–8.

[41] Such a widows list is reported to have existed in the church in Rome under Cornelius in AD 250. This list records that the church was supporting more that 1500 widows and afflicted persons. See Eusebius's *Church History* Book VI Chapter 43.

support they received in their upbringing. It would appear reasonable to accept such a passage as evidence of the expectation of social responsibility found in the early church. The issue of long-term care for older people is a significant social issue in the UK. The work that millions of people do in caring for a partner or family member who is older and in need of support, either within their own home or a family member's home, is remarkable, and it can be a tremendous silent burden to a family. But the emphasis of Paul's teaching here regarding the care of older people, whilst acknowledging the responsibility of family members in the care of the individual, does not exclude the wider church from supporting in this endeavour. Mounce notes of verse 8, which can appear particularly difficult to the person struggling over the issue of the provision of care, that there is an emphasis on the corporate sense:

> 'faith' here can have both a personal and a corporate sense: those who do not accept familial responsibilities have disowned their own personal faith, and they have also disowned the Christian faith in that they have brought reproach upon it.[42]

We have a fundamental calling upon our lives as Christians to care for older members of our family, such as parents or grandparents. But in our increasingly individualized society, with its familial breakdown and mobility of population, this is difficult, as one may not be in relationship with parents, or be separated by distance, or have parents who may reject an offer of care. However, such reasons do not provide an excuse not too offer or to at least try, as Paul writes, to 'put [our] religion into practice'

---

[42] Mounce, *Pastoral Epistles*, p. 286.

(1 Timothy 5:4). It is something that I sincerely hope I will try and do for my own parents, as difficult as it might be. Christianity is not a faith of individuals, and, as Mounce observed, there is a corporate sense to this responsibility to demonstrate care. This responsibility of the individual to care does not mean that the church is able to abdicate its responsibility from helping and enabling members to provide care. Being a carer is a hard job for everyone involved, and with our ageing population it is going to be an increasing dilemma for many families. Providing support groups, visiting, organizing practical rotas for issues like transporting people to church and generally sharing in the common burden of care will be vital for the church that desires to impact its local community over the next couple of decades. For such Christ-like compassion in action will not only impact recipients of care, but those who are carers and who need care from the body of Christ to encourage, sustain, and help them.

There is one final aspect upon which the Pastoral Epistles are silent. Gordon Harris observes, importantly, that they contain no thought of retirement from church leadership. 'Instead, elderly members remain a key to the success of the Christian movement. Old age brings some transitions but decreasing responsibility is not one of them.'[43] In Chapter 1 I recalled my experience of meeting Bishop Moses Tay, who served as the first Archbishop of South East Asia, and his description of his retirement as having been 're-tyred'. For Bishop Moses 're-tyrement'

---

[43] Harris, *God and the Elderly*, p. 89. Gordon Harris develops a number of ideas about older people and the New Testament. Chapter 6 is worth careful thought and study, particularly as it is one of the first clear examples of a theologian attempting to tackle the issues of gerontology and theology in the pages of a single book.

meant a time of *new* opportunities, not *no* opportunities to serve God.

While it is important that we have a sense in which leaders pass on the baton of leadership to new generations, the use of a statutory retirement age does not always help in such a process. It sets a fixed point that men and women work up to, only then handing on the baton of leadership. It would be interesting to explore how churches could enable their leaders through the mentoring of new younger leaders to gradually pass on responsibility to new generations. Rather than be faced with some fixed point at which leadership must change, leaders should be encouraged to look for God calling them out of their current role and into new territory as an older person. Similarly, a challenge to younger leaders taking on new leadership responsibilities would be to not view their predecessor as obsolete, but instead to enable him or her to engage in whatever God may call them on to next, whether in active ministry amongst the church or active ministry amongst their family.

5

Ageing in the Early Church

Exploring how older people were cared for and viewed by the early church is of great help as we try and carry forward into our present situation that which we can see in Scripture. Some of my own research has involved examining the fourth-century church, particularly the work and writings of Basil of Caesarea and John Chrysostom. This fourth-century viewpoint is a good place from which to look back and examine how the church sought to apply teaching regarding older people. With no explicit teaching on the subject of old age in the New Testament it must be assumed that for men such as John Chrysostom and Basil the need was to identify both the thread of teaching that runs implicitly through the Old and New Testaments and then hold this against the prevailing attitudes of the society in which they served, taught and led.

Prevailing attitudes meant that old age was generally considered negatively. While the physical experiences of old age differed, older people faced various negative physical stereotypes, and the spectre of poverty was always nearby. Our consideration of biblical perspectives identified amongst various themes the role of older people in leadership and the need to care for older people, both of which were carried forward in the life of the developing church. Christian teaching regarding social responsibility was not to be merely paid lip service, but it was to be enacted. It is possible to see the beginnings of an enactment outside of the New Testament era. In an echo of the commandment in Jesus' teaching, 'love your neighbour as yourself' (Mark 12:31), the first-century text the Didache[1] contains the same call to social responsibility:

> Do not turn away from him who is in want; rather, share all things with your brother, and do not say that they are your own. For if you are partakers in that which is immortal, how much more in things which are mortal?[2]

The second-century theologian Tertullian wrote in his *Apology* chapter 39, observing the growth of Christianity and its influence, and providing a picture of the 'organised community of Christians':[3]

> We have our treasure chest. On the monthly collection day, if he likes, each one puts in a small donation, but only if it be his pleasure and only if he is able: there is no compulsion: all is voluntary. These gifts are piety's deposit fund, to support and bury poor people, to supply the wants of boys and

---

[1] A rudimentary church manual, having originated sometime between the era of the New Testament and the developed church of the second century.

[2] An online text of the Didache can be viewed at < www.newadvent.org/fathers/0714.htm >. The Didache recalls the actions of the apostles: 'All who believed were together and had all things in common; they would sell their possessions and goods and distribute the proceeds to all, as any had need' (Acts 2:44–5).

[3] F.H. Stead, *The Story of Social Christianity* Vol. 1 (James Clarke, 1924), p. 70.

girls destitute of means and parents, and of old persons now confined to the house ...[4]

Sources such as the Didache and Tertullian suggest that the early church put its teaching into practice. The provision of social welfare was expressed practically through congregational collections, such as the one mentioned by Tertullian, which enabled direct provision for vulnerable older people. This social welfare included arranging burials and supporting older people when disability through age, whether physical or mental, prevented them from leaving their homes.

The images of older people portrayed in narratives such as Luke's Gospel and the instructions in the Pastoral Epistles regarding the lifestyle of the older person also find echoes in a declaration of Justin Martyr of *c.* AD 150. Justin claimed that he could produce from every race disciples of Christ who from childhood to the age of 60 or 70 had kept themselves pure.[5] Older people who had lived lives with Christ were held up as witnesses of purity to their society, a society which itself failed to offer such a picture of the older person.

Provision for Older People

Demetrios Constantelos in his book *Byzantine Philanthropy and Social Welfare* provides a useful text in exploring this practical outworking of social welfare that is expressed in the early Christian church (although he principally focuses

---

[4] Ibid.
[5] Ibid. p. 58. Stead quotes from Justin's *Apology* chapter 67, where Stead observes he: 'attests to the philanthropy and social unity of the Christians ...'

on the Eastern church).[6] He observes that in the ancient
Greek world philanthropy was principally anthropocentric; however, in the light of Christianity, its expression
was to be theocentric: 'The principle of philanthropy was
the love of God rather than the love of man.'[7]

This outworking of social welfare, philanthropy, was
institutionalized from an early period. The local bishop
was normally entrusted with the administration of local
institutions and so was responsible for the character of
the church. A bishop's expression of philanthropy was to
care for orphans as a parent and widows as a husband.
With the invalid he was to commiserate, and to the
stranger, give shelter. For the hungry a bishop was to
provide food, for the thirsty he was to give drink, the sick
were to receive visitation, and the prisoner was to be
given assistance. Particular attention and special support
were given to orphans, the elderly, the sick, and those
families with many children,[8] as these groups were seen
as being especially vulnerable.

In the fourth century this philanthropy took on new
dimensions as it was extended to believers and unbeliev-
ers alike, an extension recognized by Emperor Julian in a

---

[6] D.J. Constantelos, *Byzantine Philanthropy and Social Welfare*
(Rutgers University Press, 1968). Though most useful, Constantelos does display at times an overly optimistic picture
of Byzantine philanthropy, and with this perhaps the philanthropy of the early church.

[7] Ibid. See pp. 10–11 about the movement from anthropocentric
to theocentric under the influence of Christianity's development. Quoting Mark 10:45 and Matthew 20:48, Constantelos
pictures the philanthropist becoming a servant, as God
became a servant, at the heart of this being the salvation of
mankind. Therefore Constantelos states: 'Here, then, is the
basis of altruism, selfless love, Christian philanthropia.'

[8] Ibid. pp. 14–15.

letter to the High Priest of Galatia.[9] The fourth century was to be the period in which large-scale founding of philanthropic institutions was to be witnessed in the Greco-Roman Empire. F.H. Stead points to the Council of Nice in AD 359, which ordered that a home for strangers, a *xenodochium*, be opened in every city.[10] There arose other institutions to provide various forms of assistance: orphanages, *ptocheia* (houses for the poor), hospitals, and, most notably, *gerocomeia* (homes for the aged).

The coming together of church and state in the fourth century with the conversion to Christianity of Emperor Constantine was to be a powerful dynamic in the practical development of social welfare by the church, of which the provision of homes for the aged was a part.[11] The existence

---

[9] Ibid. p. 16. The letter contained a complaint from Emperor Julian that Christians were not only extending their philanthropies to people of their own faith but also to followers of the Olympian gods as well. Constantelos notes that in a letter to Arsacios, High Priest of Galatia, Julian complains: 'It is disgraceful that ... the impious Galileans support not only their own poor but ours as well.'

[10] Stead, *The Story of Social Christianity* Vol. 1, pp. 102–3. Constantelos observes this aim was also to find a declaration in the words of John Chrysostom, who urged people to set aside rooms in their own houses and receive their fellow men who needed shelter. To offer hospitality to a stranger was to offer it to Christ – a hospitable house is a xenon of Christ: from Chrysostom's sermon 45 'In Acta Apostolorum', quoted in Constantelos, *Byzantine Philanthropy and Social Welfare*, p. 185.

[11] J.G. Davies, *Daily Life in the Early Church* (Lutterworth, 1952), p. 11. Davies observes that the conversion of Constantine meant persecution was no longer an imminent reality and eased tension between church and state, enabling, in part, the rapid development of philanthropic institutions.

of *gerocomeia* underlines the church's commitment to vulnerable older people and reflects a clear need for support to be provided in old age. The church combined with the state and private individuals to establish such homes.[12] The need to care for people in old age appears to have been accepted in Imperial circles, and institutions such as the *gerocomeion* in Constantinople would have existed during John Chrysostom's time as bishop there. The oldest-known *gerocomeion* was in Constantinople, in the Psamathia quarter, and was known by this name. It is recorded that Helen, the mother of Constantine the Great, established it. Similarly, Emperor Marcian and his wife Pulcheria[13] later established a home for the aged, once again demonstrating the coming together in philanthropic action of church and state.

A director of a gerocomeion was known as a gerocomos, gerotrophos, gerocomicos or gerodocomos, and as early as the fourth century a director of a home for the aged was a highly respected person, likely to become a patrician or to be elevated to the Episcopal throne.[14] His bishop, who was the legal overseer of the charitable institutions of his diocese, would have generally supervised the work of the gerocomos.[15]

---

[12] Constantelos, *Byzantine Philanthropy and Social Welfare*, pp. 222–3. It has been possible to establish the names of at least 30 different *gerocomeia*. These were known to exist in many cities including the capital and many were named after their founders. Constantelos notes that other sources speak of many more, but identification is difficult.

[13] Ibid. See pp. 223–5 for a discussion of those persons who erected various *gerocomeia*.

[14] Ibid. p. 239. Constantelos notes: 'A fourth-century bishop of Trimithous in Cyprus, named John, had been a gerocomos, a patrician, and a physician before he was elected a bishop.'

[15] Ibid.

John Chrysostom's and Basil of Caesarea's commitment to social welfare is reflected in their sermons, writings and actions.[16] This commitment included the oversight of institutions for the aged. How they viewed older people and their needs and expectations will be the content of the next two sections, which will look at each man in turn. Examining the response of the early church to older people may inspire churches today to recover the same commitment to all people in the household of God.

John Chrysostom on Old Age

> St. John Chrysostom will always stand as a brilliant example of a bishop consumed by his sense of duty, justice, and love toward his fellow man … The famous patriarch was fully conscious of the social responsibilities of the church, finding time not only for religious services and private study but for personal ministration to the needs of the less fortunate. He tended the sick, the orphans the widows, the prisoners, and those in distress. Chrysostom built charitable institutions, such as hospitals and old-age homes.[17]

This opening description helps to set the scene for a discussion of John Chrysostom, who died in AD 407 aged 52. He rarely spoke of himself in his writings,[18] therefore directly identifying his attitude towards his own ageing process is a difficult task. However, his commitment to social welfare, including a concern for the aged, was a vital part of his service and an integral part of his theology.

---

[16] Ibid. p. 93.

[17] Ibid. p. 71.

[18] C. Baur, *John Chrysostom and his Time* Vol. 1 (Sands, 1959), p. xix.

In a sermon on charity Chrysostom wrote: 'relieve yourselves from the burden of sins through philanthropia ...
be charitable that you may receive charity'.[19] It is when one
begins to examine Chrysostom's writings in general that
the processes of ageing and his attitudes towards the
aged are revealed.[20] He acknowledges negative physical
attributes associated with old age, speaking of old age as
bringing 'a wrinkle', of the weakness of bodies that have
grown old, and of age causing people to 'fall down'.[21]
Additionally, Chrysostom warns that 'If thou hast beauty
and bloom, the approach of old age withers it, and takes
away that joy.'[22] Such negative observations do not
colour the whole of Chrysostom's view regarding old age,
though they are instructive in describing physical condi-
tions associated with the onset of age, and may be the
closest we come to his attitude towards his own ageing.

There is a great deal of material to be found in which
Chrysostom makes reference to old age itself or to older
people in general. A difficulty that can occur when
making reference to Chrysostom's use of the terms 'old
age' and so on is his tendency to use these when speaking

---

[19] Constantelos, *Byzantine Philanthropy and Social Welfare*, p. 24.

[20] All the following references to Chrysostom's writings are
from the *Nicene and Post-Nicene Fathers*, available via the
Internet (Wheaton College, < www.ccel.org/fathers2/ >).
Follow this hypertext link and click on the relevant volume
number, homily and verse [in square brackets].

[21] Vol. 14, *Homilies on the Gospel of St John and the Epistle to the
Hebrews: Homilies on the Epistle to the Hebrews*, Homilies 28 [15]
and 32 [6]. See also Vol. 9, *On the Priesthood, Ascetic Treatises,
Select Homilies and Letters, Homilies on the Statutes: Homily
against Publishing the Errors of the Brethren* [1].

[22] Vol. 9, *On the Priesthood, Ascetic Treatises, Select Homilies and
Letters, Homilies on the Statutes: Homilies Concerning the Statutes*, Homily 16 [14].

not only of people but also of the 'Law' or the old life prior to new life in Christ. There are instances where he refers to the Law as having become 'aged' or of taking on the characteristic of 'old age',[23] which in itself is once again a fascinating glimpse of the deterioration Chrysostom may have associated with the process of ageing.

The call to purity and 'right behaviour' in old age is a theme Chrysostom pursues. He writes:

> For I perceive that not only the young are mad, but the old also; about whom I am especially ashamed, when I see a man venerable from his white hairs, disgracing those white hairs, and drawing a child after him.[24]

and:

> For the hoary head is then venerable, when it acts worthily of the grey head; but when it plays youth, it will be more ridiculous than the young. How then will you old men be able to give these exhortations to the young man when you are intoxicated by your disorderliness?[25]

Chrysostom also speaks of the premature onset of old age caused by the lifestyles of those who would indulge themselves: 'For gout soon fastens upon them, and untimely palsy, and premature old age, and headache, and flatulence,

---

[23] Vol. 14, *Homilies on the Gospel of St John and the Epistle to the Hebrews: Homilies on the Epistle to the Hebrews*, Homilies 9 and 14.

[24] Vol. 14, *Homilies on the Gospel of St John and the Epistle to the Hebrews: Homilies on the Gospel According to St John*, Homily 58 [4].

[25] Vol. 14, *Homilies on the Gospel of St John and the Epistle to the Hebrews: Homilies on the Epistle to the Hebrews*, Homily 7 [8].

and feebleness of digestion, and loss of appetite, and they require constant attendance of physicians.'[26]

Chrysostom's concern about the witness of those with 'grey' hairs to the younger develops in several ways. First, there is a concern regarding 'purity', suggesting the need to be distinctive to what otherwise might be seen or portrayed of older people in the surrounding culture. Second, the concern Chrysostom expresses suggests the power of 'witness' elderly people possessed within the community. And third, the issue of witness is of significance to Chrysostom as he writes specifically on this subject, possibly responding to a situation where older people were not being witnesses to Christ. An important aspect of his concern regarding the 'witness' of older people is that it also suggests their importance to Chrysostom. In the following section of the same homily, Chrysostom expresses what he considers Scripture to present regarding old age:

> this doctrine is not my own, but Scripture also recognises the same distinction. 'For,' it says, 'honourable age is not that which standeth in length of time, and an unspotted life is old age.' (Wisd. iv. 8, Wisd. iv. 9.) For we honour the grey hair, not because we esteem the white colour above the black, but because it is a proof of a virtuous life; and when we see them we conjecture therefrom the inward hoariness.[27]

For Chrysostom it is the quality of a person's life that matters. His concern is to distinguish that living a long life

---

[26] Vol. 9, *On the Priesthood, Ascetic Treatises, Select Homilies and Letters, Homilies on the Statutes: A Treatise to Prove that No One Can Harm the Man Who Does Not Injure Himself* [8].

[27] Vol. 14, *Homilies on the Gospel of St John and the Epistle to the Hebrews: Homilies on the Epistle to the Hebrews*, Homily 7 [9].

is not itself evidence of living an honourable life, for he writes just prior to this distinction:

> I say not these things as accusing the old, but the young. For in my judgement they who act thus even if they have come to their hundredth year, are young; just as the young if they be but little children, yet if they are sober-minded, are better than the old.[28]

Chrysostom's concern for virtue and his stressing that older people did not necessarily present a virtuous life appears to have led him to move away from the use of the term 'old age' as signifying that 'an unspotted life is old age ... because it is proof of a virtuous life'. Instead, Chrysostom employs the term 'full age' to identify those who by the quality of their lives display virtuousness in old age.[29] It is little wonder he would prefer to use a different term, when in regards to a man who debases himself with his love of money, Chrysostom's observes: 'He will sit by flattering wicked people, and oftentimes depraved old men, that are of much poorer and meaner condition than himself; and will be insolent and overbearing to others that are good and in all respects virtuous.'[30] Chrysostom's desire to look for a maturity of faith, marked by the term 'full age' rather than only the outward appearance of age, could be a useful distinction in our contemporary setting, where steadily increasing numbers

---

[28] Ibid.

[29] Vol. 14, *Homilies on the Gospel of St John and the Epistle to the Hebrews: Homilies on the Epistle to the Hebrews*, Homily 8 [6] and [7]. Chrysostom states this 'full age' as 'not of nature, but of virtue'.

[30] Vol. 14, *Homilies on the Gospel of St John and the Epistle to the Hebrews: Homilies on the Epistle to the Hebrews*, Homily 15 [7].

of older people who become Christians will have had no prior contact or understanding of Christianity, and therefore will have lifestyles and understandings that share little with a life lived with Christian virtue.

This issue of affirming yet also questioning the older person is shown in Chrysostom's statement in his *Homilies on the Epistle to the Hebrews*:

> We say not these things against all [old persons], nor is our discourse against old age simply (I am not so mad as that), but against a youthful spirit bringing dishonour on old age. Nor is it concerning those who are grown old that we sorrowfully say these things, but concerning those who disgrace the hoary head.[31]

Old age is to be revered; yet it can also be brought into disgrace. A simple expression of this is found in Chrysostom's *Treatise on the Priesthood*: 'you will speedily teach them that understanding is not to be estimated by age, and the grey head is not to be the test of an elder ...'[32] To be of old age in fourth-century Christianity was not in itself evidence of virtue or leadership. For Chrysostom, a person could, during the course of his life, have laboured in the lowest rank of ministry and have reached extreme old age. Yet he would not receive reverence or promotion merely on account of age, for he could arrive at that time of life and still remain unfit for higher office.[33]

---

[31] Vol. 14, *Homilies on the Gospel of St John and the Epistle to the Hebrews: Homilies on the Epistle to the Hebrews*, Homily 7 [9].

[32] Vol. 9, *On the Priesthood, Ascetic Treatises, Select Homilies and Letters, Homilies on the Statutes: Treatise on the Priesthood*, Book 2 [8].

[33] See Chrysostom's discussion in ibid., Book 3 [15].

Just as Chrysostom expected behaviour from older men that reflected their role as witnesses of Christ, he expected the same from older women. Referring to 1 Timothy 5:9–10 and the age stipulation for widows to join the official list he states:

> It is not her own doing that she is threescore years old. Therefore he [St Paul] does not speak of her age merely, as if she has even reached those years, she may not yet, he says, without good works, be reckoned among the number.[34]

The existence of 'good works', which implies 'virtue', was necessary for the enrolment of the older woman as a widow on the canonical widows list: old age itself was not sufficient for inclusion. Such a list is likely to have continued into the fourth century. Considering the various roles of older women in the early church, J.N.D. Kelly refers to the historian Palladios's (*c.* AD 365–*c.* AD 425) recollection of Chrysostom's 'summoning the brigade of widows' in Constantinople. For Chrysostom to be able to 'summon' them there must have been widows on the canonical list. Kelly observes that from the fourth century deaconesses were often drawn from this canonical list of widows.[35]

Older women often faced a society that considered them as highly negative stereotypes, such as alcoholics, or as women of ill repute. Against such a backdrop of restricting attitudes Chrysostom makes further reference to the actions of women in old age. In his *Homilies on the*

---

[34] Vol. 13, *Homilies on the Epistles to the Galatians, Ephesians, Philippians, Colossians, Thessalonians, Timothy, Titus, and Philemon: Homilies on the First Epistle of St Paul to Timothy*, Homily 14.

[35] J.N.D. Kelly, *Golden Mouth: The Story of John Chrysostom – Ascetic, Preacher, Bishop* (Gerald Duckworth, 1995), p. 122.

Epistle of St Paul to Titus, in a reference to Titus verse 3, Chrysostom states:

> For this was particularly the vice of women and of old age. For from their natural coldness at that period of life arises the desire of wine, therefore he directs his exhortation to that point, to cut off all occasion of drunkenness, wishing them to be far removed from that vice, and to escape the ridicule that attends it. For the fumes mount more easily from beneath, and the membranes (of the brain) receive the mischief from their being impaired by age, and this especially causes intoxication. Yet wine is necessary at this age, because of its weakness, but much is not required.[36]

Not only does Chrysostom note the frailty of old age requiring the necessity of wine, without providing any reason apart from that of an apparent 'natural coldness', he also refers to the 'ridicule' that can accompany drunkenness, describing it as a 'vice'. Such a description is understandable if Chrysostom was developing his expectations of the role and actions of older people against the backdrop of a society that often portrayed older women as alcoholics. His response suggests that this stereotype of women in old age was not new, being similar to the situation about which Paul gave instruction to Titus.

This leaves us in a slight quandary as Chrysostom both criticizes and reveres older people. The key to understanding Chrysostom on old age is to place him firmly into the context he emphasizes: that the economy of this world and the divine economy of God are utterly different and operate under differing values. Therefore people,

---

[36] Vol. 13, *Homilies on the Epistles to the Galatians, Ephesians, Philippians, Colossians, Thessalonians, Timothy, Titus, and Philemon: Homilies on the Epistle of St Paul to Titus*, Homily 4.

including those in old age, are somewhere on a journey between those two economies. The success or failure of this journey is marked by the person's virtue, or lack of it. The journey to the divine economy is not simply the process of growing old. Chrysostom is clear. White hair and old age are no indicators of virtue. However, those who are of old age and experiencing the distinctiveness of the divine economy will be living where old age is valued, contrary to the values of the worldly economy they had journeyed from. It is a timely message for all of us that, regardless of our age, we do not complete our journey with Christ until we meet him face to face. There is no part in our journey prior to that point of arrival where one can sit back and consider oneself to have reached the goal.

Chrysostom also regrets those who do not reverence age,[37] and in his *Commentary on St John* he brings out the distinctiveness between the economy of this world and the divine economy regarding age: 'In things of this life the young man is useful, the old useless; "but in Mine," He saith, "not so; but when old age hath come on, then is excellence brighter, then is manliness more illustrious, being nothing hindered by the time of life." '[38] Chrysostom identifies in his teaching that there is a difference to be seen between the fourth-century world's understanding of old age and that of the church. In the former, the old are considered useless; in the latter,

---

[37] Vol. 14, *Homilies on the Gospel of St John and the Epistle to the Hebrews: Homilies on the Gospel According to St John*, Homily 87 [4].

[38] Vol. 14, *Homilies on the Gospel of St John and the Epistle to the Hebrews: Homilies on the Gospel According to St John*, Homily 88 [1]. This is in reference to John 21:18, where Jesus tells Peter the death he would face when in old age.

old age can mark excellence and manliness without hindrance. Chrysostom expresses this benefit of age in a slightly different way in the following statement: 'The young indeed look forward to a distant old age; but we who have grown old have nothing but death to wait for.'[39] It is helpful to add to this comment on death a separate observation made by Chrysostom: 'there is no old age there, nor any evils of old age, but all things relating to decay are utterly removed, and incorruptible glory reigns in every part'.[40] This is not Chrysostom in older age resigning himself to the reality of death, but embracing the promises of heaven, where all things relating to decay will indeed be utterly removed.

In his description of Flavian, Bishop of Antioch, travelling to the Emperor Theodosius on behalf of the city, Chrysostom identifies the limitations and possibilities of old age. He speaks of Flavian venturing his life for his flock by journeying to the Emperor, though, as Chrysostom notes, there was much to keep Flavian in Antioch:

> first, his time of life, extended as it is to the utmost limits of old age; next, his bodily infirmity, and the season of the year, as well as the necessity for his presence at the holy festival; and besides these reasons, his only sister even now at her last breath! He has disregarded, however, the ties of kindred, of old age, of infirmity, and the severity of the season, and the toils of the journey; and preferring you and your safety above all things, he has broken through all these restraints. And,

---

[39] Vol. 9, *On the Priesthood, Ascetic Treatises, Select Homilies and Letters, Homilies on the Statutes: Treatise on the Priesthood*, Book 1 [5].

[40] Vol. 9, *On the Priesthood, Ascetic Treatises, Select Homilies and Letters, Homilies on the Statutes: An Exhortation to Theodore after his Fall*, Letter 1.

even as a youth, the aged man is now hastening along, borne upon the wings of zeal![41]

This description of Flavian's journey illustrates the negative and positive aspects to be found in Chrysostom's references to old age: the worldly effect of bodily limitation, yet the divine effect of carrying an elderly man along in his zeal. In his homily concerning the return of Flavian we see the portrayal of a man in old age considered virtuous. Chrysostom observes:

> He took not his age in account; and he dispatched this long journey with just as much ease as if he had been young and sprightly ... a single old man, invested with the priesthood of God, came and moved the heart of the Monarch ... the favour which he bestowed upon no other of his subjects, he granted to this one old man ...[42]

Chrysostom presents a picture of old age that is influenced by both society and Christianity. One would go further and suggest that much of his writing regarding old age takes an almost 'apologetic' theme, as he differentiates between those who would disgrace their old age and those who grow old in Christ. However, his concern for virtue and purity is not driven purely by a desire for control; Chrysostom's concern to deal with the respect due to older people would answer any charges of being an avowed disciplinarian. John Chrysostom's concern was for where people were journeying to and the promise of heaven:

---

[41] Vol. 9, *On the Priesthood, Ascetic Treatises, Select Homilies and Letters, Homilies on the Statutes: Homilies Concerning the Statutes*, Homily 3 [1].

[42] Vol. 9, *On the Priesthood, Ascetic Treatises, Select Homilies and Letters: Homilies on the Statutes*, Homily 21 [16].

Let us believe him, and lay hold on that in which there is no vanity, in which there is truth; and what is based upon a solid rock, where there is no old age, nor decline, but all things bloom and flourish, without decay or waxing old, or approaching dissolution. Let us, I beseech you, love God with genuine affection, not from fear of hell, but from desire of the kingdom.[43]

Basil of Caesarea on Old Age

Here was a man who was both a Christian pastor and an embodiment of hellenic culture, an aristocrat and a monk, a theologian and a diplomat, a shrewd, perhaps at times unscrupulous political operator but also a saint.[44]

In Basil of Caesarea we again meet a leader of the early church who was a man influenced not only by Scripture but also by the desire to present Christ to the culture that surrounded him. This culture influenced his understanding of and therefore his teaching about old age. Basil conducted a significant social programme that was not born out of purely practical need and, similarly to Chrysostom, he found himself driven from a theological understanding:

If you have not been merciful, you will not receive mercy; if you have not opened your house to the poor, you will be

---

[43] Vol. 13, *Homilies on the Epistles to the Galatians, Ephesians, Philippians, Colossians, Thessalonians, Timothy, Titus, and Philemon: Homilies on the First Epistle of St Paul to Timothy,* Homily 15. See Chrysostom's reference to 1 Timothy 5:20.

[44] P. Beagon, *Social and Political Aspects of the Career of St Basil of Caesarea* (Unpublished DPhil Thesis, Oxford University, 1990), p. 262.

locked out of the Kingdom of Heaven; if you have refused bread to the hungry, you will be deprived of life eternal.[45]

For Basil soteriological concern was tied to action and not merely words, action driven by a divine requirement. Witnesses such as his younger brother, Gregory of Nyssa, attest to the extent of Basil's concern for people from all backgrounds:

> when on a certain occasion a severe famine afflicted both the very city in which he happened to be living and all the land which was tributary to the city, selling his possessions and having changed the money into food, when it was rare even for those who were very well supplied to prepare a meal for themselves, he continued during the whole period of the famine to support both those who came together from all sides ...[46]

In the provision of social welfare by the early church (from the fourth century until the time of Justinian in the sixth century) deaconesses were used, which is recorded in Basil's *Epistle 105*.[47] This use of deaconesses in the practical outworking of the church is significant for the role of older people, if, as was mentioned in the ministry of John Chrysostom,[48] deaconesses were commonly drawn from the official list of widows, which had clear age stipulations regarding membership. Therefore it could be reasonably

---

[45] Quoted in Constantelos, *Byzantine Philanthropy and Social Welfare*, p. 21.

[46] *Encomium of Saint Gregory, Bishop of Nyssa, on his Brother Saint Basil, Archbishop of Cappadocian Caesarea*, Sister J.A. Stein (tr.) (The Catholic University of America, 1928), pp. 37–8.

[47] Constantelos, *Byzantine Philanthropy and Social Welfare*, p. 85.

[48] Kelly, *Golden Mouth*, p. 122.

suggested that Basil actively used older women in the social outreach of the church, an activity that played a central role in the church's mission in the fourth century.

Perhaps the most famous of Basil of Caesarea's philanthropic institutions was the Basileiados, built outside the city of Caesarea, which combined a range of buildings for the care of the sick and the destitute, and distributed food to those in need.[49] The institution was described as 'a new city, a storehouse of piety, the common treasury of the wealthy ... Where disease is regarded in a religious light ... and sympathy put to the test.'[50] One of the most significant difficulties in examining Basil of Caesarea's social provision for older people is the holistic nature of this programme, which is well expressed in the following prayer attributed to Basil:

> [O God] ... rear the infants ... support the aged ... accompany those who voyage; journey with those who journey; defend the widows; protect the orphans; free the captives; heal the sick. Remember, O God, those who are under trial, and in the mines and in prison, and in bitter labours, and in all affliction, distress and tribulation.[51]

Basil's social programme clearly encompassed older people, both in physical provision and possibly through the

---

[49] P. Rousseau, *Basil of Caesarea* (University of California Press, 1994), p. 139.

[50] This description is from Gregory Nazianzenos is quoted in Constantelos, *Byzantine Philanthropy and Social Welfare*, p. 154. There is further reference to the Basileiados in the *Encomium of Saint Gregory*, Stein (tr.), p. 45: 'what a tabernacle of testimony even as regards the body he provided outside the city ...'.

[51] Constantelos, *Byzantine Philanthropy and Social Welfare*, p. 282. This prayer is commonly accepted to be part of the 'Liturgy of St Basil'; however, it may be of a later date than Basil himself.

active involvement of older women who were widows, in the expression of social care to those in need generally.

However, we can see further expression of his attitude towards older people in Basil's writings to his ascetic communities. Many of these communities were in the forefront of Basil's provision of social welfare and the teaching received by older and younger members of the communities would have found expression in their own attitudes towards the aged to whom they gave support. Basil decreed that monasticism should not be divorced from the needs of society and the practice of social welfare. He encouraged the monks of his communities not only to take care of the needs of those who surrounded them inside the walls of the ascetic communities, but of all people, and to compete with each other in works of charity.[52] One of Basil's communities was placed alongside his Basileiados and the monks provided for those who required the institution's services. These monastic centres performed many different tasks in social welfare. Palladios chronicles an example of two wealthy sons of a rich businessman distributing their inheritance to charities. One of these sons founded a monastic centre, which was to become a place for the stranger, the sick, the poor, and the elderly.[53]

In Basil's instructions to his ascetic communities there was a clear role in leadership for those who were older. The superior was the leading figure of the community, who was considered responsible for discipline and the pastoral

---

[52] Ibid. p. 88.
[53] From Palladios's *Historica Lausiaca*, quoted in Constantelos, *Byzantine Philanthropy and Social Welfare*, p. 94. The actions of these two sons, and many people like them, were influenced by the models of leaders such as Basil of Caesarea and John Chrysostom, who distributed their wealth before entering the service of the early church.

care of monks in his charge.[54] There were clear criteria as to the person who should fill the role of superior, and these criteria included that of 'age'. In the selecting of a superior, Basil wrote, 'let regard be had to his age as a factor in deciding whether he have the honour. For it is natural for men to pay greater respect to elder men.'[55]

Basil conditions such an appointment with concerns regarding people of old age similar to those of John Chrysostom's. Basil writes of a proposed superior:

> I think it necessary to investigate his life and see not only whether he is old in years, for it is possible to have a juvenile character along with grey hairs and wrinkles, but especially whether his character and manners have grown old in decorous fashion, so that all he says and does may be a law and a rule to the convent.[56]

Once again, it is possible to see a familiar theme of linking age and virtue, though always qualified by the two not being synonymous. The expectation is that the older person would hold the personal qualities necessary to be in leadership in these ascetic communities of the fourth-century church. This is reflected again in Basil's instructions regarding how a superior should be disciplined. Basil instructs that those 'who being foremost in age and understanding correct the superior'[57] so that 'good order be not impaired, such admonishment should be entrusted to those who are pre-eminent both as regards years and wisdom'.[58] It was not appropriate for those of

---

[54] W.K.L. Clarke, *The Ascetic Works of St Basil* (SPCK, 1925), p. 39.
[55] Ibid. p. 135.
[56] Ibid.
[57] Ibid. p. 40.
[58] Ibid. p. 193, rule 27.

young age to correct the elder in leadership of the ascetic community.

The above instruction also provides understanding about the physical appearance of the aged. Basil's references to 'grey hairs' and 'wrinkles' appears to hold a less than flattering view of physical appearance in old age. He advises that young monks should not sleep together in the same area: 'rather have an old man between you ... Go to old men difficult of access, who anoint with their maxims the young men for deeds of virtue and who appearance cannot harm.'[59] In the case of younger sisters of the community who wished to speak to a man about an urgent matter, Basil writes that this conversation should be conducted by the superior, and 'in the presence of one or two of the sisters, who because of their life and years are able to be seen and converse without danger'.[60]

In each of these statements there is a theme regarding the lack of attractiveness of people in old age. Therefore there is no 'risk' of others being physically attracted to them. Such a view must surely have been greatly influenced by a societal rather than scriptural view of old age. A societal picture would, according to the evidence listed earlier, normally provide a pejoratively negative picture of the physical attributes of old age. However, it would be to misrepresent Basil to only state that he expressed a negative view of physical attractiveness in old age. We must add the qualification that Basil also presented a positive picture of the virtue of older people, which was a benefit to those who were younger. In the case of young monks, the older monks were those who could anoint the young monks for deeds of virtue. In the case of older sisters, it was not only due to their 'years' that they could

---

[59] Ibid. pp. 66–7.
[60] Ibid. p. 144.

converse without danger, but also because of their 'lives', which implies lives in which virtue was evidenced.

In his teaching regarding widows Basil is clear about his expectations of those women who, in their old age, had joined the official list of widows: 'a widow who has won the reputation for the good works spoken of by the apostle, and has reached the order of those who are widows indeed, should abide in supplications and prayers with fasting night and day'.[61] In his letter *To a Fallen Virgin* Basil implores the virgin to remember the example of her grandmother, 'grown old in Christ, still youthful and vigorous in virtue'.[62] Older women were seen as examples for younger members of the church.

Basil also deals with the text of 1 Timothy 5:2. Answering a question regarding the discipline of older women his response brings out some revealing thoughts regarding the physical attributes of old age and virtue and the life the older woman should be leading. Considering the issue of an older woman falling into the same sin as a younger woman, he first notes attributes of age: 'sloth is almost natural in old age, but not so in youth. Just as wandering thoughts and perturbation and audacity and the like are natural in youth but not in old age ...'[63] However, Basil weighs the consequence for the older woman falling into the sin of the younger woman: 'wandering thoughts, audacity, or perturbation, make the elder

---

[61] Ibid. p. 126, from *The Morals*, Rule LXXIV – 1. *The Morals*, or *Moralia*, are contained in Basil's work *Ascetica*. See the discussion in ibid. p. 16 for further details.

[62] See *Nicene and Post-Nicene Fathers: Series II,* available via the Internet (Wheaton College, < www.ccel.org/fathers2/ >), Vol. 8, *Basil: Letters and Select Works: Letter XLVI, To a Fallen Virgin.*

[63] Clarke, *The Ascetic Works of St Basil*, p. 261, rule 82.

woman deserve a heavier condemnation, since she is helped by her very age to be meek and quiet'.[64]

It would be unrepresentative to leave Basil on this negative note regarding old age. He, like Chrysostom, demonstrates an awareness of the difference between the worldly and the divine economy for those of old age, and how this difference was to be expressed through the virtue of the older person's life. In this, Basil gave value to the role of the older person in the continuing witness of the church. Responding to a question asking how those who have laboured long in the work of God help newcomers to an ascetic community, Basil responds:

> If they are physically strong, by showing unwearied zeal, and making themselves an example of every virtue. If they are weak, by such a condition of soul that it appears from their face and every movement that they are fully convinced that they see God and have the Lord ever present.[65]

Our Present Situation

The need for older people to live lives that are distinctive to the cultures that surround them remains as true today as over 1600 years ago. There is much that we can learn from these two leaders of the early church: the recognition of the value of the older person as a witness to living God's way; the use of older women in leadership as well as older men; the recognition of wisdom in the life of the older person; and the reality that being an older person does not necessarily mean someone is a holy person! Consider some of the issues revealed in the opening

---

[64] Ibid.
[65] Ibid. p. 303, rule 200.

chapters: the challenge of increasing sexually transmitted diseases amongst those over 65 and the changing power dynamic in society with a widening wealth and poverty gap amongst older people. The frank assessment of older people provided by these two early church leaders is a timely reminder of the scriptural reality that Ecclesiastes 4:13 observes: 'Better a poor but wise youth than an old but foolish king who no longer knows how to take warning.'

Neither Chrysostom's nor Basil's accounts are fanciful or hazy, far from the realities of old age. The negativity with which they speak of the physical experience and appearance can at times be harsh. However, there remains a certain realism of an older age that is not hidden by lifestyle or covered up by cosmetics or surgery, but instead is able to be a resource to enable the virtue of younger generations. Their teachings contain a challenge to the church today in their concern to provide for the needs of vulnerable older people, not only spiritually, but also practically. For the early church the provision of social welfare and mission were inextricably linked. The challenge for us today is to link back together that which has been divided in the church's recent history.

Perhaps the most helpful aspect to take forwards with us from the fourth century is the recognition of a sense of journey from this world to the divine. This is ultimately where we are called to in Christ Jesus, and it is this element of spiritual journey in our contemporary world that we turn our attention to next.

6

Spirituality of Older People: Contemporary Reflections

Religion or Spirituality?

The Christian church holds in its history a dynamic understanding of spiritual life and expression. The spirituality or
spiritual development of the Christian is vital in making
the journey with Christ through life, growing to become
more like him. The theologian Alister McGrath defines
Christian spirituality as being 'the quest for a fulfilled
and authentic Christian existence, involving the bringing
together of fundamental ideas of Christianity and the
whole experience of living on the basis of and within
the scope of the Christian faith'.[1] In this understanding,
spirituality and religion are delicately intertwined and not
to be separated, as one naturally flows into the other. The
identification of spirituality as the quest of the individual
is clearly held within the context of the Christian religion,
as McGrath refers to the fundamental ideas, or doctrines,
of Christianity. However, outside of the church's life,
religion and spirituality are being divided up and are
increasingly seen as incompatible. Religion is viewed as an

---

[1] A.E. McGrath, *Christian Spirituality* (Blackwell, 1999), p. 2.

expression of mass belief that has now expired along with a structuralist view of society. Instead, spirituality can be many and varied, reflecting the multitude of forms the individual may wish to choose from as he or she practises his or her 'spirituality' in a post-structural world.

Harold Koenig is a leading writer on the subject of religion and health. He observed how, at a conference of 60 leading researchers in medicine and science, it proved difficult to find definitions of religion and spirituality that were acceptable to everyone.[2] In the recent *Handbook of Religion and Health* the following working definitions were recorded from this conference:

Religion: Religion is an organized system of beliefs, practices, rituals, and symbols designed (a) to facilitate closeness to the sacred or transcendent (God, higher power, or ultimate truth/reality) and (b) to foster an understanding of one's relationship and responsibility to others living in a community.

Spirituality: Spirituality is the personal quest for understanding answers to ultimate questions about life, about meaning, and about relationship to the sacred or transcendent, which may (or may not) lead to or arise from the development of religious rituals and the formation of community.[3]

There are two key elements to pick out from these definitions. The first is the way religion is understood as impersonal, with references to systems, symbols and rituals. Though it is also defined as community relationship, this 'living in community' is commonly understood as

---

[2] H. Koenig, M.E. McCullough and D.B. Larson, *Handbook of Religion and Health* (Oxford University Press, 2001), p. 17.
[3] Ibid. p. 18.

representing the institutional and structural. The second element is the identification of spirituality as a personal quest that may or may not lead to an experience of community, which it could be completely separate from. These suggested definitions are strikingly different from a traditional Christian understanding. The implications of their existence cannot be ignored, and have not appeared in some little-known text that will hardly ever be taken off a library shelf, but in a key and highly significant academic text that will impact and influence continuing research in this area.

This distinction between spirituality and religion has entered gerontological research and has been recently expressed by the Australian gerontologist Ruth Bright. She writes:

> We must not confuse spirituality with formal religious observance and it was interesting to find, in a book of interviews with elderly Australians, how few of them spoke of formal spiritual creeds or a belief in life after death, yet how many spoke of belief in a creator spirit of the universe.[4]

This stark contrast between spirituality and religion may sound alien to many Christians. However, it is a present and relevant debate in which the church, especially the evangelical tradition, is not offering a distinctive understanding of religion and spirituality as being interconnected. Individualism, about 'me' and 'my' preferences, has poured over into the life of the church. We are in the process of dismantling the interconnectedness of religion and spirituality in the life of the church by default, as we fail to engage in the contemporary debate of those who would seek to define our community. The word 'religion'

---

[4] R. Bright, *Wholeness in Later Life* (Jessica Kingsley, 1997), p. 55.

is about the fellowship of believers who share faith in Jesus Christ our Lord and Saviour, who meet together and who celebrate their life as part of the body of Christ. But we are losing this meaning to those who would define it only as formal institutions or structures, and so dismiss 'religion' as being about power and control, not liberation or freedom. So the church recoils from 'religion' and is left with 'spirituality', but outside of the church this is now defined by the individual who may pick and choose the expression of his or her 'spirituality' according to personal preference. Therefore the consumer church is created out of a reactive fear rather than a proactive vision that entrusts the future church to the one who holds the past, present and future in his hands.

The tragedy is that this is an area into which many older Christians could speak, sharing how religion and spirituality combine in a life lived, but their voices are not lifted up, encouraged or enabled within the local and national church. Consider the witness of older people that we have seen through Scripture and in the early church: they lived their lives constantly reconciling their past, present and future in a way that a younger person simply cannot. To enable these older voices and to rejoice in them, not merely paying them lip service, daring to stand alongside them saying 'yes' and 'amen' to their witness of Christ by lives lived journeying with him – what a glorious testimony to the blessing of religious fellowship and spiritual transformation that would be in our nation. Think of how John Chrysostom marvelled at the witness of the elderly Bishop Flavian travelling and gaining access to see the emperor in Rome. Consider Justin Martyr writing, again to an emperor. Who did he use as examples of lives lived with Jesus? Older men and women. And remember Basil of Caesarea imploring the younger virgin to follow the example of her grandmother in how she lived her life.

How marvellous it would be to enable older men and women in our churches to live lives that shine as beacons for people to follow. How wonderful it would be to help them express these lives to others while encouraging younger people to look at these beacons for direction in their own journeys of ageing. But in many ways the eyes and heart of the church have been seduced by the allure of youth. It fails to acknowledge the beauty of age, and for this there is a price that is being paid.

In her book Ruth Bright considers why so many older Australian people offered a view of spiritual rather than formal religious beliefs. She asks whether this distinction could have occurred because the person was alienated from God by religious teaching early in his or her life, or through a life in which tragedy and suffering were often seen, and in which God became remote as one who could not understand or be understood.[5] Her findings not only emphasize the growing distinction between religion and spirituality, but also the way in which older people are not turning to traditional religious forms to provide meaning in later life. Attending the second International Conference on Ageing, Spirituality and Wellbeing in Durham, UK, in July 2002, I heard one main speaker explain the way in which the word 'spirituality' had come out of Christian theology and practice, but had now become a universal code word to be used cross-culturally and in a secular context. Offering a definition of spirituality, the same speaker suggested it as 'creating an oasis of the soul', linked to a sense of space with the older person grounded in a particular spirit spot, a description from Native American spirituality. The spirit spot was a place for recreating self. In the debate of religion or spirituality, the prevalence of thought is toward spirituality that excludes a traditional

---

[5] Ibid.

religious understanding. This is not being dreamt up by academics separated from the rest of the world, but is rightly reported as research conducted into the lives and attitudes of older people.

There is a gross myth that has gained prevalence in modern Christian thought that older people either 'return' to the church or in some way become 'more' spiritual as they age, so becoming more open to specifically Christian belief. There are two aspects to this myth of older people and they lead to only one place: exclusion. First, older people are often taken for granted and missed in mission; they do not hear the gospel proclaimed and explained to them. Second, the older person's spiritual needs in continued growth in Christ-likeness, maturity of faith, exploring questions and developing in prayer are excluded because they are 'overlooked', like the 80-year-old lady mentioned in Chapter 4. Our current pioneers of the third age grew up in an age where doubt and questions were not to be publicly expressed. For many it is as they reach the end of life that all the unanswered 'buts' and 'what ifs?' rise to the surface of their minds and hearts in the realization of the finite nature of life and the infinite nature of knowledge. Being old does not mean that a person automatically has great spiritual strength or depth. Basil of Caesarea knew this in the fourth century when he observed that a man may have grey hairs on his head but could still have a juvenile character! Spiritual strength and depth develop in a life spent journeying with Christ, growing with others in the body of the church.

Facing the question of the interaction of age and spirituality is vital. What does it mean? What are the positives and negatives? In considering the question we might start to see that there is an inherent value in the spiritual life of the older person who has journeyed long with Jesus, but that a long life may also bring greater difficulty, need and uncertainty in tackling questions of life. Taking time to think about these aspects is important because it leads us to begin to recover the value of the spirituality of older people and the value of spiritual investment in older people. If we invest now then we will be preparing people to not only hand over the baton of faith to emerging generations, but also enabling the older person to face the finality of life on this earth with an expectation of eternal life with Jesus. At the same conference mentioned earlier one of the speakers presented the following challenge. If young people want to have a meaningful old age it would be good if they learnt to respect and love older people. If they see no meaning in older age they will become another example of self-fulfilling prophecy and find no meaning in their own old age. Recovering the importance and value of spirituality in the body of Christ for the older person will reap the reward of enabling future generations to age with greater confidence in Christ and so in turn pass on their own baton of faith.

The Implications of Old Age

Older age does not mark a period in which life experience and adaptation become static forces in the life of the individual. Simon Biggs, a gerontologist, observes of the development of self-perception in old age that:

> On the one hand, there is an inner urge to preserve continuity in the face of constraint in the outside world, on the other hand, new requirements might lead to different ways of relating to the world which again has to come to a workable comprise with the dominant social reality.[6]

---

[6] S. Biggs, *Understanding Ageing: Images, Attitudes and Professional Practice* (Open University Press, 1993), p. 52.

The author and priest Gerard Hughes develops this theme of reconciling the inward perception and outward reality in a Christian context. He observes:

> In youth, most of us are full of dreams, hopes and ambitions. We set our hearts on fulfilling these dreams, but relentless reality keeps frustrating us. Even if we do succeed in fulfilling some of them, becoming wealthy or successful, we may find that we have worn ourselves out, damaged others and lost our friends and family in the process, and the success turns to ashes in our mouths. With failing physical strength, we no longer have the energy or ability to pursue what once gave us life, and we are left to contemplate our own emptiness. Even if we have been religiously committed people, we may find that in old age we are assailed by doubts about faith, and that God disappears as our physical energy abates.[7]

For Hughes there is a positive element, as he sees nature allowing the older person to benefit from stillness in older age, and in that stillness he sees the opportunity to listen to God.[8] Not everyone shares Hughes' more positive view of old age as granting an opportunity to listen to God. A more standard view that Hughes identifies is that as people age they are assailed by doubts about faith and God starts to disappear. This certainly would appear to follow the experience in older Australians detailed by Ruth Bright.

In an interview Richard Ingrams reflected on his own career as an editor, satirist and creator of the magazine

---

[7] G.W. Hughes, 'Is There a Spirituality for the Elderly? An Ignation Approach' in A. Jewell (ed.), *Spirituality and Ageing* (Jessica Kingsley, 1999), p. 16.

[8] Ibid. p. 17. Hughes observes this forced opportunity to listen as blessing, not a curse, highlighting the psalmist's call to 'Be still and know that I am God.'

The Oldie and observed one of the dangers of old age: 'You've got to watch it, I think. I find myself becoming much more tolerant in old age.'[9] It is this aspect of increasing tolerance that is important. Ingrams viewed his younger days as a time of intolerance and of seeing everything in 'black and white'.[10] Here echoes of Hughes's observations start to appear. Tolerance is not marked as a point of greater understanding and therefore greater certainty. Instead tolerance is a description of greater doubts and greater uncertainties involved in life. The need for the older person is to begin to come to a workable compromise with society, an inward perception which not only includes the physical and the emotional, but also the spiritual, as dominant ideologies, including that of faith, come under increasing scrutiny.

It is perhaps the theologian Margaret Guenther who comes closest to this experience when she reflects on her own second half of life, writing, 'we are able to embrace ambiguity. I am stunned when I realise how little I know and how every year I seem to know less and less.'[11] This knowing less and less may seem an astonishing statement from a woman who has lived much of her life as an academic. However, there is great insight to be gained from this point as regards the spirituality of the older person. It is not that one may rely on greater certainty in spiritual understanding; instead there is a need to support the older person as they face greater uncertainty. As Guenther goes on to observe:

---

[9] S. Jenkins, 'Old Enough to Know Better', *Third Way*, March 1999, p. 17.

[10] Ibid.

[11] M. Guenther, *Toward Holy Ground: Spiritual Directions for the Second Half of Life* (Darton, Longman & Todd, 1996), p. 7.

The knowing that characterises the second half of life is open to mystery, drawn to the depths, and ready to risk. It is not easily distracted by minutiae. The questions it raises are rarely multiple choice or true-false. Embracing ambiguity leads to a kind of holy agnosticism, a comfortableness with mystery and open-endedness. It is the time we begin to ask ourselves: What do I really know? What matters? What is the rock-bottom of my faith?[12]

In her observations Guenther writes from a liberal theological background, in which one may argue that the individual would normally encompass a certain level of ambiguity in his or her belief system. It is also a theological background in which the idea of divine mystery finds expression in both doctrine and liturgy. There is little evidence, at present, to identify the difficulties that older people from more conservative backgrounds face theologically as they age, though the ability to encompass ambiguity and be comfortable with this would appear to be a useful tool for the older person seeking to reconcile the finite nature of age and the infinite nature of knowledge. Guenther's observation of an increased open-endedness in the second half of life is suggested by research presented at the 1998 Lausanne Consultation on Nominality. A report on Protestant decline in Costa Rican churches observed that of those over 60 years of age who had left the Protestant church the largest group gave open-ended answers to questions about their leaving.[13]

---

[12] Ibid. p. 8.

[13] J.I.G. Varela, 'The Costa Rican Experience: Protestant Growth and Desertion in Costa Rica: Viewed in Relation to Churches with Higher Attrition Rates, Lower Attrition Rates, and More Mobility' in H. Wraight (ed.), *They Call Themselves Christian* (Christian Research, 1999), p. 49.

Uncertainty about one's faith is not something the church should run away from: it is a healthy expression of what it means to grow old.

I recently had the opportunity to spend a few hours with Gerard Hughes discussing these matters. He observed that as people age they begin to see things in a new way and can experience doubts that younger generations do not understand. Many older generations weren't allowed to have doubts, difficulties with an aspect of worship or doctrine, and doubts about matters of faith were a definite no. Faith was often seen as to assent to the creed. But merely speaking some words and assenting to a statement of faith is not faith! St Paul was clear that 'if you confess with your mouth, "Jesus is Lord," and believe in your heart that God raised him from the dead, you will be saved' (Romans 10:9). Speaking words for many older people has only provided a veneer that has been built up over the years, which is then eroded by the realities of older age and death. In discussion, Hughes described spirituality as being the exploration of the transcendent God, of which the context for the Christian is the ontological fact that we live in the Spirit. It is the Spirit of God who is able to sustain the older person through the uncertainties of age, as it is through the Holy Spirit that the love of God, which is able to drive out all fear, is poured into our hearts (Romans 5:5; 1 John 4:18).

In approaching the spirituality of older people we grapple with the difficulty raised by the actual chronological age of the person, as the individual attempts to reconcile the past, present and future of his or her life. It is perhaps how the issue of the past comes into focus that raises the greatest challenge. Metropolitan Anthony of Sourozh summed this up from his own experience:

I write not from an objective point of view but just as an old man, now in my eighties, and from the personal experience I have gained both as a physician and as a priest within the last 50 years. The problems of the old can be centred on the past, present and the future. One of the things that an old or ageing person has to face is his own past. It applies to people and it applies to nations. I think it was Solzhenitsyn who said that a nation which has not come to terms with its past cannot resolve any problems with its future. This applies to us all; as long as we turn away from our past, close our eyes, do not want to remember, we cannot resolve problems in the present or the future.[14]

Anthony of Sourozh places his observations in the context of his life experience, in this instance fifty years working as a physician and priest. Guenther, Hughes and Ingrams also provide similar contexts to their observations of their present state, that is, old age. One could question whether or not a person's chronological age and spirituality can really interact in this way. However, time and again it is possible to see that chronological age and the process of growing older do have a direct impact upon the spirituality of the individual. Reconciling inward and outward experiences, realizing the limitations of old age, in emptiness, in ambiguity, in tolerance, and coming to terms with the past – these take place in the context of a person's chronological age, for one needs to have lived long enough in order to face such questions and gather such experiences.

But how do we understand the value of the older person, the role of his or her life experience combined with existing spiritual belief, or the way his or her life

---

[14] Metropolitan Anthony of Sourozh, 'The Spirituality of Old Age' in Jewell, *Spirituality and Ageing*, p. 30.

experience impacts a fresh expression of a spiritual life? While some commentators seek to rebut the potential benefit of faith in the older person's life, seeing it as an inhibiting factor, others have identified benefits for the individual. Professor Peter Coleman has carried out a growing body of work in this area and has observed the following: 'Religion is one of the great providers of meaning to life ... religious thinking constitutes one the most prominent and successful ways older people control their emotional responses in difficult situations.'[15] Coleman has also noted the way in which the individual's perception of him or herself appears to culminate in later life, and so calls for opportunities to be made available for reconciling differing patterns of life.[16] If we combine the observation that religion can provide a successful mechanism in ageing and the call for provision for the reconciliation of life, there is a tremendous opportunity for the church to speak into the life of the older person in ways that are beneficial to his or her continuing process of ageing. But in order to do so we need to be challenged to see the value of spirituality in the life of the older person, and then enabled to respond.

Recovering Spirituality

It has been argued that coming to terms with one's own mortality is a major life task,[17] and old age is indeed a

---

[15] P. Coleman, 'Adjustment in Later Life' in J. Bond, P. Coleman and S. Peace (eds), *Ageing in Society* (Sage, 1993²), pp. 129–30.

[16] Ibid. p. 130.

[17] E.C. Bianchi, 'A Spirituality of Aging' in L.S. Cahill and D. Mieth (eds), 'Aging', special edition of *Concilium* Vol. 3 (SCM Press, 1991), pp. 58–9.

period in which the individual is faced with both the immediacy of his or her own mortality and the mortality of friends and family. There is a tendency amongst some writers to see old age merely as some transitory phase during which the individual is either purely coming to terms with his of her past or looking to his or her future death. However, this devalues the experience of old age itself. Yes, there is a process of reconciliation, but there is also a process of living in the present. It is at this point of the 'present' that the challenge needs to be put that older people are not the church of 'yesterday', just as younger people are not the church of 'tomorrow'. Rather, we are all part of the church of *today*, and it is in this present context that the value of the spirituality the older person brings to the life of the church community needs to be recovered. If this value is recovered we could begin to see older people as witnesses of virtue in a society in which virtue has become a shifting commodity and older age devalued.

In 1969 K. Richards made the call to enable older people to experience 'the adventure of living' and, quoting Paul Tournier, wrote: 'this casting off, this ever-increasing purging away of activity, this passage from the order of doing to the order of being, which is the law of old age, is also an adventure'.[18] I wonder how much of an adventure growing old is truly viewed as? An adventure is both exciting and stimulating, but how many older members of churches are also considered to be 'adventurers', and how many consider themselves to have such a title? There is an urgency to enable older people to experience a life in the 'today' of this adventure. Twenty-two years on from 'the adventure of living' E.C. Bianchi observed the changing patterns of a technological society and the need to recover

---

[18] K. Richards, 'The Adventure of Living', *Contact*, May 1969, p. 15.

spirituality for people who are middle-aged and are increasingly faced with being driven into intense and competitive action:

> I envision elders who have worked through the transitions of mid-life becoming even more intensely concerned about great issues of ecology, peace and justice. Such elders would return, in different ways, to the centres of decision-making and of service. But technologic culture pushes the old to the periphery of society, encouraging them to live out their 'golden years' in pursuits of individualistic consumerism.[19]

In recovering spirituality the Bible contains a variety of models and experiences, both of the older person who has lived a life of faith, and of the older person who is new to an expression of faith. Each model displays the value of older people as examples of people who are distinct from the societies in which they have grown old and who, having been pioneers in the process of ageing, are witnesses to Christ. Scripture does not treat the aged as a single homogeneous group – there are many different portrayals, some positive and some negative. In the early church this value of older people in Christ continued through witnesses, models of virtue and exemplars. Yet there was also a healthy pragmatism that spirituality was not always synonymous with old age. Early church leaders were to look for evidence of the virtue of the older person and were concerned to correct and challenge older people who were not presenting a witness of Christ. While such challenges may be seen by some as 'telling people how to behave', they also reveal the great value of older people to church leaders concerned with the mission of the church in their society.

---

[19] Bianchi, 'A Spirituality of Aging', p. 59.

There is much to be applied to our present situation. Margaret Guenther, writing from her own theological background, provides a helpful observation of her desire for a guide in the ambiguity of her own old age. To this end Guenther embraces the idea of a saint, in her case Anna, the supposed mother of Mary. Guenther's desire was to embrace a role model, someone who could help her to express what it meant to be a woman experiencing old age: 'as I felt myself grow older, I felt drawn to the idea of the amma, the old mother, to the concept of maternal love separated from procreation and physical birth-giving'.[20] Guenther's comments illuminate what it feels like to age and trying to find a point of reference in Christianity through which present experiences could be reconciled. As Guenther goes on to observe later, there are no 'Annas' in our popular culture: 'her brand of wisdom is not at home in the pages of popular magazines ...The Anna of legend is strong and reliable, a source of wisdom born of long experience and closeness to ordinary human life.'[21]

It is an extraordinary state that the church has reached to not have the easily identifiable models of older people who have lived lives of faith and spiritual expression. It is not the fault of older people themselves, as many older people today received a particular view from the church and writers during their early years that taught that feelings either were not important or were to be ignored,[22] which has ultimately led to a situation where for many faith remains a private matter.

But older age is a multifaceted experience that produces multifaceted people. Some older people will be able

---

[20] Guenther, *Toward Holy Ground*, p. 12.

[21] Ibid. p. 17.

[22] A. Webber, *Life Later On: Older People and the Church* (Triangle, 1990), p. 19.

to display a depth of spirituality that enables them to reconcile their present and be a blessing to the community in which they worship. However, many others need to be enabled to experience the power of Jesus Christ in their lives and be given the freedom to express doubts in a community that supports and upholds them in their faith. But is this happening? Are older people being enabled to express and grow in their spirituality as valued members of the body of Christ? To this question I believe the present answer is no. As long as I continue to hear leaders in the church, and those training to be leaders, describing older people either as 'the problem' or as 'yesterday's church', then older people's spirituality and their potential for spiritual expression are devalued, if not denied. For this act of denial there is a heavy cost to pay in the mission of the church, one that concerns me greatly, as we are already experiencing the consequences a church in decline. Ann Webber provides an evaluation of what the church will lose if it does not begin to recover the value of the expression of those experiencing older age:

> Older people's understanding of God needs to be accepted and listened to if the aspects of his character are to be correctly understood. Then the next generation can in its turn understand, in context, God's new revelation to them. If today's older people's experience of God is ignored, future generations cannot be expected to believe that today's knowledge of God has any relevance for them. History will repeat itself.[23]

The author Beryl Bainbridge in an interview about her upbringing in the north of England reflected upon the north–south divide that exists in the UK and observed:

---

[23] Ibid. p. 25.

it's a generation gap that separates the North from the South, the past from the present. My generation has much in common with those hill sheep recently culled in Wales. It is said that over time the doomed animals had acquired an inherited memory of how far they could graze; new flocks won't be aware of the boundaries.[24]

Old Testament material reminds us it was considered a sign of cursing to kill the older members of a household, removing their wisdom and strength and making it unavailable to the next generation. Recovering the spirituality of older people in the present and valuing people who express this enables future generations to learn where the boundaries are in life and in faith. The older members of our churches hold our inherited memory – we ignore them at our own risk.

Emerging Opportunities

John Drane has emphasized the need to recognize that many people today are on a spiritual quest. No longer do we see people happy to accept a traditional status quo that presents Christianity as a series of facts to be believed. People want relevance and practical answers to the hard questions of life and to belong to a place that is interested in them and who they are.[25] The mistake that is made is to assume that the older person is not on that quest, considering the older person to represent the status quo, rather than desiring relevance and practical answers. To

---

[24] From an essay by Beryl Bainbridge entitled 'Up North' in the Saturday *Times Magazine*, 18 August 2001.
[25] J. Drane, *Cultural Change and Biblical Faith* (Paternoster, 2001), p. 121.

view older people as unaffected by the spiritual search of younger generations is quite wrong. The church's recent focus on researching youth culture has been beneficial in uncovering its multifaceted nature. However, the church has never inquired about older culture, hence the assumption that older people are in some way mono-faceted, which is nonsense. Perhaps a more helpful view would be to consider the truth that older people have paved the way for what has happened since – such developments do not happen in a vacuum. Pioneers broke the ground before the settlers followed, and these pioneers have found themselves desperately trying to figure out what it means to live longer than previous generations ever did, with a better quality of life, greater opportunity, and more time to reinterpret life and its meaning.

One of the most striking examples of differing understandings of religious/spiritual belief seen recently was in an article on the popular Third Age web site, entitled 'Spirituality in the Third Age'. Sylvia Boorstein, a writer on the subject of spirituality, explained her own view that 'Life's truth is in the moment ... I am a Buddhist, and I am a Jew ...'[26] In this extraordinary statement, which sees a combining of two religions that are polar opposites into one expression of spirituality, a challenging example of religious syncretism beginning to be expressed amongst older people is presented, and an incredible opportunity is revealed. The challenge will come in the discipling of older people, where there will be an increasing need to be able to deal with people who have developed in a multi-cultural, multi-faith and media-driven society, in which people have been encouraged to construct what they

---

[26] C. Reeve, 'Spirituality in the Third Age'. This article can be viewed at < www.thirdage.com/features/healthy/spiritual /index.html > (accessed 14 May 2002).

would like to believe. The opportunity is that spiritual matters have not dropped from the agenda. We are not a wholly secular society, refuting the existence of anything other than the human mind: pure rationalism has been rejected.

A practical example of this new spiritual search amongst people of all ages was presented in a recent article in the *Health Service Journal*, which opened with the following statement:

> At a time when formalised religious observance is diminishing in the UK, interest is growing among health-care professionals in matters religious and spiritual. New-age and complementary therapies are flourishing, the number of NHS chaplains has more than doubled, and there is interest in the spiritual duties of healthcare staff, particularly nurses, in relation to patient care.[27]

The opportunities are out there: they only need to be grasped!

---

[27] J. Swinton and S. Pattison, 'Come all ye Faithful', *Health Service Journal*, 20 December 2001.

7

Implications: Working with Pioneers

Working with pioneers of the third age brings us to the place where theory and practice must meet. How can we take what has been outlined in the previous six chapters and begin to apply it for the benefit of our pioneers, that we might continue to grow the kingdom through mission and discipleship from generation to generation? It is easy for theory and practice to miss each other either by remaining talking points that never meet or by engendering such a sense of wonderment over what to do that it never looks possible they could meet!

I experienced this 'lack of meeting' when during a conference reception, at which I was giving a short presentation on gerontological issues, I was asked the following question: 'How can a younger person help disciple an older person?' I would love to write that in that room of people I gave a brilliant and erudite response, but I can't. Instead, I made a fundamental error. I spoke as a gerontologist and forgot that I am also a pastor. I responded only in the language of theory and left a bewildered questioner wondering what I had just said! It was only on the train home later that day that I realized what I should have said. A younger person can help to disciple an older person by joining his or her journey of life and faith and respecting the territory this older pioneer has already traversed, by being willing to listen and learn about this journey, and by being prepared to speak about the continuation of the journey with anticipation, so walking it together.

Discovering the Journey

The context of the journey comes close to the ideas expressed in Chapter 6 of the need for an older person to reconcile past, present and future. Theorists put this into the language of developmental psychology, describing the need for the individual to know some kind of reconciliation toward life itself, so enabling him or herself to transition the developmental stages into older age. However, the pastor can use this theory of life reconciliation and identity to explain the need to not only to be reconciled to one's life, but also to Christ. For the journey that we are each on is towards him who is the author and perfecter of our faith.

In his recent book *The Journey* Alister McGrath explores this theme of journey through a series of metaphors. Creating a picture, McGrath writes:

> Imagine … You are on a road. It stretches far into the distance, before you and behind you, before disappearing over the horizon. As you make your way along this long and often lonely road, you may find yourself wondering what lies behind the horizons. What has been left behind? And what lies in the distance? With this thought, we come to one of the great themes of Christian spirituality – *remembering and anticipating*. It is a way of thinking which helps us to keep going along that road.[1]

---

[1] A. McGrath, *The Journey: A Pilgrim in the Lands of the Spirit* (Hodder & Stoughton, 1999), p. 23.

This sense of journey, containing the processes of remembering and anticipating, is a tremendously helpful image. For McGrath this journey is marked by the great biblical theme of exodus and he observes the way in which each one of us, regardless of our age, is engaged in journeying from our own Egypt to the Promised Land.[2] During that journey we remember the land from which we have travelled and anticipate the promise of life with Christ in heaven that awaits us beyond our physical death. We could also add to this theme of exodus the theme of reconciliation. The Hebrews were rescued from their captivity in Egypt and led by God on an exodus for 40 years through a land of desert, during which they were increasingly reconciled in relationship with him as God led them into the land that he had promised them. So it is on the journey from our own Egypt to life with Christ. It is a process in which reconciliation needs to be enabled and recognized – reconciliation to God through Jesus Christ our rescuer and redeemer, and reconciliation to our past and our present – so that we might be able to leave behind the land from which we have travelled, awaiting with anticipation the new land that is promised us.

In Chapter 2 it was observed that for many today the desire to cling to life has meant that death has remained firmly as the last great taboo. The image of the hearse arriving in the night, or the economic, medical and physical pursuit of longevity at all costs, combine to demonstrate the simple truth that many people cannot leave their Egypt. And where some have begun their exodus journeys, they grumble in the desert as their hearts harden, for they have been unable to reconcile past and present so that they might know anticipation of the land that lies ahead. In his exploration of this journey, McGrath

---

[2] Ibid.

calls upon the resources of various writers for illustration, including the eighteenth-century minister Jonathan Edwards:

> We ought not to rest in the world and its enjoyments, but should desire heaven ... We ought above all things to desire a heavenly happiness; to be with God; and dwell with Jesus Christ. Though surrounded with outward enjoyments, and settled in families with desirable friends and relations; though we have companions whose society is delightful, and children in whom we see many promising qualifications; though we live by good neighbours and are generally beloved where known; yet we ought not to take our rest in these things as our portion ... We ought to possess, enjoy and use them, with no other view but readily to quit them, whenever we are called to it, and to change them willingly and cheerfully for heaven.[3]

In this illustration Edwards offers a challenging perspective on life. How tightly do we cling to this life? As a minister, how well do I enable older people to have a loose hold on the things that are temporary, so that they might take hold of that which is eternal? The portrait Edwards paints is one in which life is clearly lived actively and enjoyably, a portrayal which rings true for many experiencing their third age. In the midst of activity and opportunity, death would seem to be failure, or at least a process through which the individual is 'robbed' of life. However, for the older man or woman experiencing the frailty of his or her fourth age, with increasing disability and the presence of death through the gradual failure of his or her physical body, the question of how tightly one clings on to life

---

[3] Jonathan Edwards, *The Christian Pilgrim*, quoted in ibid. pp. 46–7.

would seem to be inappropriate. But the reality of the matter is that questioning how tightly one clings to life is perhaps even more urgent at this stage of an individual's life. Paul wrote in 1 Corinthians 15 'Where, O death, is your victory? Where, O death, is your sting?' But one can cling to life so tightly that the increasing threat of death's sting is an unbearable consideration. In fact, so tightly can one hold to life, either for comfort or security, from guilt, anger or sadness, from pleasure or simply enjoyment, that the thought of letting go becomes impossible. Yet the promise of our journey to Christ is to enter into a land even better than the one we know now. For there, God will wipe every tear from our eyes, there will be no more death, no more pain, for there the present order of things will be no more.

The use of journey as an image does not automatically imply activity, as observed from Gerard Hughes in Chapter 6, for in the process of ageing and entering the frailty of older age activity may no longer be possible. The priest and gerontologist Elizabeth MacKinlay has described this later stage of old age as a time when being becomes more central to living than doing.[4] In our world, where value is derived by what we do and the roles that we carry out, we have reached the point where we have forgotten that God created us as human *beings* and not human *doings*! This has tremendous significance for the older person who through illness or developing frailty finds him of herself no longer able to be active, so losing his or her role, position and status not only in the sight of the skewed value systems of our society but more importantly in his or her own eyes. MacKinlay acknowledges that some older people have a good self-awareness and satisfaction with life, which carries them through the

---

[4] E. MacKinlay, *The Spiritual Dimension of Ageing* (Jessica Kingsley, 2001), p. 12.

trial of disability, loss and isolation. However, she observes of other older people that signs of despair are demonstrated as they grow older.[5] MacKinlay's focus is on the opportunities and possibilities for spiritual intervention in clinical practice situations, but there are opportunities for intervention in other areas of life crisis for the older person. At a recent conference Professor Peter Coleman observed how for many older people bereavement was potentially one of these key crisis points. Research conducted by Coleman and his team found that over time older people were leaving the church, not joining it. Reported in the media in 2000, Coleman presented his findings to the British Society of Gerontology. Over 20 years, following a group of 340 older people, the number for whom religion was important had dropped from three-quarters to less than half.[6] Further research by Coleman has revealed a key disappointment for older people as the failure of the church to offer support at the crisis point of bereavement. The people Coleman and his team were interviewing were not wanting extensive support following bereavement but revealed disappointment that they had not received something as simple a follow-up visit after a funeral to see how they were coping. The opportunity is for the church to demonstrate Christ's compassion to the older person in crisis and/or experiencing frailty and to journey with the person in this painful point of his or her life in which questions about the meaning of life are often faced alone.

In journeying with pioneers we engage with people, we share in their experiences, their travel, and their

---

[5] Ibid.

[6] One of the articles that picked up this news story was B. Summerskill, 'Elderly Lose Faith in Religion', *The Guardian*, 3 September 2000.

exodus from Egypt. Those who work in ministering too, discipling the older person, have the blessing of having the potential to reflect the glory of God with an unveiled face into the life of the person with whom they engage. Moses led a people through 40 years with compassion, determination, faith and hope, and he too was being transformed, as he aged during the journey. Enabling someone who is older to be a disciple, to journey alongside him or her, is to listen to and share in the story of his or her own journey. It is a process that does not leave the younger accompanier unchanged, as he or she also can draw closer to Christ and be transformed through the journey.

Latent Spirituality

The funeral service remains one of the few areas where most church ministers talk to more people who aren't Christians at a significant level than at any other point. The 'journey of life' is an image I have used for funeral addresses and the use of 'journey' can be a helpful image for many people, as it speaks both to those who know Christ as redeemer and reconciler, but also to those older people who are outside of the Christian faith. I have been consistently amazed at the way people receive the idea of journey and appreciate the recognition of their own spiritual search. In the context of a funeral address the image of journey is one into which the question of 'where are we travelling to?' can be placed. Chapter 2 focused on the changing scene that an ageing population brings and identified that there remains in our society a latent spirituality. We are not a purely rationalistic society that sees only the potential of the human endeavour to bring advancement and answer questions of life and the universe. There is an increasing spiritual quest afoot, affecting people of all ages, and Chapter 6 looked briefly at the way in which this is seen in gerontological debate as academics and practitioners struggle to seek a definition of religion and more particularly 'spirituality'. The search for an adequate and measurable definition of spirituality and/or religion has been resisted for many years, but it is significant that a growing number of academics have acknowledged the vitality of belief in the life of the older person, and the need to understand the implications of such belief. Sociologist Grace Davie observes of people of all ages that: 'The crucial point to grasp is that some sort of religiosity persists despite the obvious drop in practice. The sacred does not disappear – indeed in many ways it is becoming more rather than less prevalent in contemporary society.'[7]

Those who accompany our pioneers on their journeys must take in that there will be increasing numbers of older people for whom religious or spiritual beliefs have been constructed to reinforce self-identity. In a world of information about a variety of beliefs and practices, the pluralistic self will be one of the questions needing to be answered in both mission and discipleship. A mix-and-match belief system is not a recent phenomenon. Callum Brown observed the way in which pre- and post-war people who demonstrated religious belief would often also hold local superstitions as significant in their lives as well. However, the greatest change between past super-stitions and present spiritual constructions is the amount of information with which people are equipped to make personal choices in their beliefs.

Chapter 2 contained a discussion of this issue, identi-fying the generational breakage of the transmission of

---

[7]　G. Davie, *Religion in Britain Since 1945* (Blackwell, 1994), p. 43.

faith, of the alienation of men and especially women from the church, and the way in which secularization as a more recent phenomenon has taken hold. Despite this rapidly changing picture I firmly believe that, while we can see the way in which popular culture and religious practice and belief have become separated, there remains a latent desire for spiritual expression. Much is made at present of the decline of the church. It has been reported at numerous points in the national media and has received the attention of various organizations, speakers and conferences. It seems at any and every opportunity we are reminded of the onslaught of the secular against the sacred. Many of these dire pronouncements have been swallowed whole by a church desiring to stir up missionary zeal at all costs. This is not to decry mission: it is central to who we are as Christians, and the endeavour of mission is at the very heart of the church, for we have good news to proclaim. My concern is that the focus of churches has been taken from reaching out with the good news of Jesus to people of all ages and instead only giving attention to the need to reach young people. To reach younger generations is vital, but the consequence of an unbalanced approach will be to repeat the failure of previous generations that never prepared older members to pass on the baton of faith and leadership, because they didn't know how. Callum Brown's experience of being shut out of 1970s Glasgow youth clubs by generations who didn't know how to cope will be repeated again. Alienation between young and old will continue in the body of Christ as each generation fails to understand and relate to the other, because neither embraced the process of ageing itself.

Build the Household of God[8]

I was recently talking with an older member of another congregation and listened as he explained how his church had decided to become generationally focused, concentrating its resources to reaching and discipling people in the 20–30 age range. I heard how many of the older members of this church were leaving to join other local churches. This hadn't come from division or anger, but simply from a pragmatism that the needs of the older believer were no longer going to be met in that place. In fact, the release of these older members was described as a potential blessing to many other places, which is ultimately true. But hearing this story raised again for me a concern as to what it means to be members of the 'household of God'. Paul writes to the church in Ephesus 'you are no longer foreigners and aliens, but fellow citizens with God's people and members of God's household' (Ephesians 2:19). First, the use of 'household' speaks of family and of community. Second, it speaks of diversity: male and female, old and young, poor and wealthy, Gentile and Jew. All who are in Christ are 'being built together to become a dwelling in which God lives by his Spirit' (Ephesians 2:22). There would appear to be strength in diversity, not only diversity of activity amongst peers, but also of age. Looking at the Old Testament in Chapter 3 it was seen that to live into old age was considered to be a sign of God's blessing and that older members of a family were considered to bring strength and wisdom to their people.

---

[8] I am grateful to Adam Sparks of the Evangelical Alliance for the use of his unpublished essay 'Church Family? Intergenerational Tension in the Church' as background to this section.

If we are building churches that do not contain older people through the active choice of leadership, are we weakening our household by removing from it the strength and wisdom of age? My concern may be unfounded, but it is based on the following questions. Are we building households that will last, that have the diversity of age to ensure that faith, knowledge and memory are passed on from one generation to another? What will happen in the generationally focused church when people in one generation leave it and pass on into another, simply on account of the process of their own ageing, which they cannot prevent? Will we encounter younger people crying out for pioneers who could show them the way as they tread new territory in their own lives?

We hear of the growth of the 'I' in society. Some commentators have suggested that to reach out with the gospel to an increasingly fragmented society we need a church that is fragmented and customized to the needs of the individual. Toward this end, much has been made of the word 'tribalism' in work with specifically younger generations, recognizing a society that is fragmented into 'tribes'. However, it is a splendid misappropriation of this sociological concept merely to apply it to younger generations of people. The social philosopher Michel Maffesoli, seeking to describe the break-up of mass culture, developed the term 'tribus' to describe a key social aspect of contemporary living represented by cohesion through identity politics, lifestyle cultures, and so on. A helpful note is provided in Rob Shields's Foreword to Maffesoli's *The Time of the Tribes*:

Typical examples of tribus are not only fashion victims, or youth sub-cultures. This term can be extended to interest-based collectivities: hobbyists; sports enthusiasts; and more important environmental movements, user-groups of state services and consumer lobbies.[9]

Shields continues by explaining that the term 'tribus' could also be applied to Canadian senior citizens lobbying to use national park facilities and to the National Riflemen's Association in the USA.

If we are to use 'tribal' in its correct sense in seeking to engage in mission we would surely aim to have churches formed from all kinds of differing agendas and identities. Tribalism is not only relevant for younger people but for people of all age categories and identity groups. However, it is hard to find a description of the church in the New Testament that would support such a construction. The early church contained many differing tensions, of which generational tension was but one, but it consistently represented the church as both a unity and diversity held together in Christ by the Spirit.

Richard Niebuhr in his classic book *Christ and Culture* recognized the need to engage in cultural work, observing how Jesus sent his disciples to do this. By engaging in cultural work Niebuhr did not see Jesus as bringing people into only a reflection of the existing cultural forms. Instead, 'In his single minded direction toward God, Christ leads men away from the temporality and pluralism of culture.'[10] If tribalism were to be applied across the generations we would end up with churches fragmented according to age, attempting to reach out to a fragmented society, therefore only able to rescue people from one experience of fragmentation to another, and

---

[9] R. Shields, Foreword, in M. Maffesoli, *The Time of the Tribes: The Decline of Individualism in Mass Society*, Don Smith (tr.) (Sage, 1996), p. xi.

[10] H.R. Niebuhr, *Christ and Culture* (Faber & Faber, 1952), p. 53.

so failing to lead people away from temporality and towards God.

Building the household of God containing people of all ages undoubtedly brings us into areas of difficulty: dealing with generational tension within a congregation; encouraging older members to reach out to younger and vice versa; discipling people who are older than leaders and so on. These are all costly endeavours in time, energy, prayer, love and forgiveness, and often require a tough skin! But the cost of excluding the older person from evangelism to discipleship is the removal of potential strength and wisdom from the household – a precious and valuable asset. As Ann Webber observed, 'If today's older people's experience of God is ignored, future generations cannot be expected to believe that today's knowledge of God has any relevance for them. History will repeat itself.'[11] The tragedy of our present situation is that history is about to repeat itself. The older person's knowledge of God can be ignored, often without realization, or left to the 'old people's groups', which can be subconsciously viewed as some kind of elephant's graveyard!

Robert Best has described the potential of older people as 'beacons of hope', seeing older adults as presenting living hope that replaces fleeting wishes. 'Elders have learnt deferred gratification, the ability to postpone pleasure for the sake of long-term satisfaction. They are able to provide a vision of what is yet to be, and a sense of hope. They understand the value of planting now and reaping later.'[12] I find this to be a tremendously encouraging vision

---

[11] A. Webber, *Life Later On: Older People and the Church* (Triangle, 1990), p. 25.

[12] R. Best, 'The Spiritual Role of the Elder in the Twenty-first Century' in D.O. Moberg (ed.), *Aging and Spirituality* (Haworth Pastoral Press, 2001), p. 27.

of potential for older people in a church that encourages people of all ages. The image of the 'beacon of hope' for Best is set in the context of the mentor relationship between an older and younger person, not merely separated in age by years, but by decades. When one considers the mentor relationships of Paul (Timothy) and Peter (John Mark), these older men demonstrated to those younger than themselves that satisfaction and hope is to be found in Christ alone, and what marvellous beacons these servants of Christ remain to us today through Scripture.

I consider myself fortunate to serve in a church that contains a healthy range of people of all ages. We aren't perfect and we don't always get the balance right, but I rejoice at the way older members are committed to reaching younger people, giving support through prayer, finances and time where they can, and the way older members of our local household have a voice to encourage younger members to remain steadfast, to persevere, and be assured that God is on their side.

Living a Full Age

The modern myth that the older a person is the holier he or she must be would be completely alien to the early church leaders John Chrysostom and Basil of Caesarea, who left us in no doubt that the older person faces challenges about the way he or she conducts his or her life, just as any younger person might. The older person who brings dishonour to his or her length of years lived or who causes a younger person to be led astray receives far stronger criticism from these early church leaders, on account of the benefit of age itself providing men and women with lives rich with experience. Using the term 'old age' alone as signifying the maturity of faith someone demonstrates could be considered misleading. Chrysostom perhaps offered a more helpful term when he described the older person who lives a 'full age' and who therefore possess virtue and displays it in his or her life as a faithful witness to Christ's transforming presence.

Admittedly, contemporary language is full of varying verbal constructions employed to describe old age, each one going in and out of fashion with remarkable speed as writers, academics and campaigners dismiss one description in favour of another. But the use of the term 'full age' could be a helpful signifier in the area of Christian living for the older person. Living into 'full age' brings ideas of living into a fullness of Christ, displaying a fullness of the fruit of the Spirit outworked in a Christian's life. 'Full age' speaks of longevity of years lived in Christ's presence, being transformed and moulded through his loving mercy. It brings an image of the continuation of journey beyond the death of our physical bodies, for it is only then that each of us will know him fully: as now we can see only dimly, then we will see face to face. Full age brings a helpful distinctive between the older person who displays Christ and the older person who does not. It is the older person who is living into full age that Basil of Caesarea and John Chrysostom uphold as a witness of virtue, and it is such people who need to be given a voice today, upheld for what their lives display as a challenge and encouragement to others.

Canon Peter Green wrote a wonderful booklet in 1950 when he was himself experiencing old age. In it he observed the way in which young boys and girls at school were told by distinguished, and older, people that their school days would be the best they would experience, leaving the realization that things were not going to get better as they got older. Reflecting upon this, Green wrote,

'How much better if one could tell them with conviction that life rightly lived goes on getting better and that God's promise to those who love Him and whom He loves is that at evening time it shall be light.'[13] Sitting in the Bodleian Library in Oxford a few years ago, I found the words of this older man a tremendous encouragement to me, as a younger person, to live my life rightly before God and to be assured by someone who had lived into the fullness of life that at the evening time of death there will not be darkness but light waiting for me. Such a description of older age was, and continues to be, a most precious gift.

The person trapped in Egypt cannot be left out of this equation, as there remains the potential for redemption and transformation for the person of any age. The challenge is how to enable this to happen. The journey of discipleship is difficult at any stage of life and the urgency that comes in later life cannot be lost. I have already referred to the way in which the younger person can accompany the older person on this journey, but the challenge here is to the older person to embrace such an opportunity. Peter Green provides further thought in this matter, describing the guiding rule for happiness for the whole of life to be the ability to develop a:

> forgetfulness of self and interest in others ... It is so easy, as we grow old, to think of our own aches and pains, our own failing strength, our own dull lives. But no one really wants to hear of these things though friends may be kind enough to listen. But other people's lives, especially young people's troubles and difficulties and joys, can always be found full of interest.[14]

---

[13] P. Green, *Old Age and the Life to Come* (A.A. Mowbray, 1950), pp. 12–13.

[14] Ibid. p. 19.

The challenge that this older man brings in his writing is to lift one's head from the immediacy of older age. Despite the reality of death and of frailty, at whatever point it is encountered, there remains the possibility to share in the journey of another and to encourage them as they encourage you. The difficulty in achieving this is in churches where younger people are missing. In these churches devoid of younger members there is little opportunity for older people to lift their heads from the immediacy of their own age and instead to reach out to enable those younger than themselves to tread the path they have already walked themselves.

I learnt an important lesson during my time working alongside adults with learning disabilities. It is all too easy to look on the outside of the person and fail to recognize the person within. Humankind looks on the outward appearance and, unlike God, fails to see the heart. So it is with those of us who are older or younger. We either see the outward appearance of a past we think is irrelevant, or a future we don't understand, and so either way miss the potential of the person. That lesson taught me a valuable prayer: to ask God to teach me to look upon the heart and never merely upon the outward appearance. It is a lesson I carry with me as I journey alongside older people in the church I serve today.

Countering the Longevity of Youth

A quest in current gerontological thinking is seeking an answer to the following question: What is successful ageing? For many the answer to this question is found in medical technology. The ability to extend life, to put off the threat of death, to extend youth and push back the onset of old age – all seem to provide the appearance of success. Yet in light of the discussion above, does success rest on only the outward appearance of vitality and activity? I hope that it does not. For otherwise it means that many older people experiencing frailty and illness are 'failing' in their ageing process, and this will be something medical technology will seek to 'correct'. Professor Tom Kirkwood observes that: 'The commonest misconceptions about the ageing process are that we age because in some fundamental way we *cannot* survive for longer, or that we are *programmed* to die. Neither of these ideas is correct.'[15] At the end of the book in which Kirkwood makes this observation he includes 'Miranda's Tale', a fictional account located in the future where technological development has ensured unlimited longevity for the individual. This short story is an examination of the way such unlimited opportunity gradually begins to be rejected by people. It is a fascinating look at the ethics associated with ever-extended longevity and, though constructed around a fictional account, it is based on theoretical research already taking place. When I enter older age myself I will probably do so later than my parents, with medical opportunities to increase my life span, sustain my levels of life activity and so maintain my 'successful' ageing.

However, the meaning of ageing, and what is more the meaning of successful ageing, does not rest in activity. As observed in the opening section of this chapter we have been created not as human 'doings' but as human 'beings'. We live in a world where we are defined by our ability actively to participate, a value prevalent in the church. But if our meaning in life is purely tied to what we do or accomplish through activity then we are leading a life of poverty. Meaning in life is at the heart of what it is to be

---

[15] T. Kirkwood, *The End of Age: Why Everything about Ageing is Changing* (Profile, 2001), p. 10.

human and this, Elizabeth MacKinlay explains, is closely tied to hope, 'and hope is essential for continued human existence'.[16] It is a dreadful existence when the only thing people can derive their value from is activity.

At the second International Conference on Ageing, Spirituality and Wellbeing, Dr Leo Missinne presented an inspiring lecture regarding the search for meaning of life in older age.[17] Missinne observed that the disease of our time is boredom, which has encouraged people to do destructive things in their life in order to feel alive. That is, boredom leads to destructive activity, as meaning cannot be found in any other place. However, Missinne presented a challenge to rediscover meaningfulness in three ways: (1) The Creative: that a person can achieve value in life by doing something, by achieving tasks, thereby creating to find meaning. (2) The Experiential: experiencing the good, the beautiful, by knowing one single human being in all their uniqueness – and knowing this means to love this person – love, beauty, truth can provide a reason to live. (3) The Attitudinal: a person may be in such distress that the previous two values do not provide meaning. But meaning and value may be realized through the way in which the person faces his or her suffering. This is the highest achievement in life – the person who is suffering can give the best lessons about life and health.

Missinne continued by challenging younger people that if they wished to have a meaningful old age it would be good to learn respect and love older people and be in contact with good, beautiful older people. For if they see

---

[16] MacKinlay, *The Spiritual Dimension of Ageing*, p. 14.

[17] Taped recordings of this lecture (and all conference lectures) can be obtained through the conference convenors, The MHA Care Group, or the Christian Council on Ageing. A book of conference lectures and workshops will be available in 2003.

no meaning of life in older age they will simply become another example of self-fulfilling prophecy and find no meaning in their own old age.

This is a powerful rebuke to those of us who would seek our value through activity alone. Missinne is right to identify our need to experience relationship, and for our attitudes to be transformed, for this is exactly what our relationship with Christ should be about. Our meaning as a Christian is not primarily or only derived from our levels of service or activity, rather our meaning is because we are 'in' Christ. We are experiencing a relationship in which we are being transformed in attitude, which is expressed where we are able by the activity of service.

The tragedy of many evangelical churches at present is that they focus primarily upon activity, upon the roles that people do in order to provide them with meaning. In doing so we ultimately see those who cannot contribute to the cacophony of activity as a drain on finite resources and so ignore the older person and celebrate the activity of youth. In fact, we find that we need younger people, for they are the ones who we suppose can provide the activity necessary to sustain and carry forward the mission of the church. In a recent review of Adrian Hastings's book *A History of English Christianity* Gerald Bray recognized as painfully accurate Hastings's assessment of evangelical-ism. Hastings writes:

> It seems characteristic of Evangelicalism both to appeal to youth and to make rather grand claims concerning its ad-vances ... Many young Evangelicals fall away or merge sooner or later with the wider believing community, escaping the grip of its too often rather juvenile theology and spirituality ...[18]

---

[18] Gerald Bray's review can be read in *Themelios* 27:3. The book reviewed was A. Hastings, *A History of English Christianity*

This is a stinging assessment of evangelicalism, which one may wish to question. However, Hastings's observations ring true when one considers the recent concentration of evangelical churches and organizations on the needs and activity of youth at the expense of older people. But this criticism also holds an opportunity. If we can work to recover the value and voice of the older person within the church, if we can encourage and enable older people both to discover meaningfulness in old age and then share this discovery with those younger than themselves, then we might offer a theology and spirituality able to sustain the believer through all the trials of life and age in his or her trust in Christ as Saviour and Lord.

We live in a society in which the search for meaning in life is tremendous and where people are increasingly discovering the poverty of value to found in activity alone. The short-lived adrenalin rush of activity may provide brief respite, but it holds no investment for a time of life where such activity is no longer possible. Our pioneers of the third and fourth ages have arrived and are asking 'Why am I here?' and 'What does this mean?' By investing in enabling them to discover these answers in the present, we ensure future generations can inherit this knowledge, which will be to our strength and wisdom.

Final Thoughts

In Chapter 4 I referred to Graham, who stood up and encouraged those younger than himself with his 50 years

---

[18] (*continued*) *1920–2000* (SCM, 2001). See p. xlv for the quotation. Hastings's assertions have been further borne out by Alan Jamieson's *A Churchless Faith: Faith Journeys Beyond the Churches* (SPCK, 2002).

of knowing Jesus Christ in his life. A few weeks ago, at lunch with Graham and his wife, Margaret, two of a number of older people we are blessed to have within the congregation we serve, Graham expressed concern about his role within the church. He had served as an elder and vice-chairman of the PCC and he felt he had been someone who had a certain spiritual authority because of these roles. However, as he was no longer active in these various roles, he felt that he had lost this authority. It is a sad indictment that we have left such precious pioneers feeling that they have no opportunity to share their wisdom and strength because they do not hold a title or role. I would never have realized how Graham and Margaret felt if they had not gently offered their present experience to me: a failure on my part. In response, I observed to these pioneers of the third age that they have a continuing place and should be given every opportunity to speak wisdom into the life of the church, simply on account of their fullness of age witnessed by the length of their pioneering journey through life led by Christ. For by their presence, contribution, and encouragement we are a household that is stronger and wiser.

And so in our consideration of these pioneers we return to the place where we started, the voice of an older woman, a pioneer of the third age:

The situation is that my generation is a pioneering generation. My mother and father didn't live as long as I will, and I've no one to show me how to grow old – we are breaking new ground as older people. Who will show us the way?

Will you?

Appendix

Ten Recommendations for the New Territory of Age

1. Be prepared to identify areas in which you have under-estimated or discounted older people. Acknowledge the existence of ageism in the life of the individual person, the local and national church, and seek God's vision of the older person as revealed through Scripture.
2. Be equipped to understand the territory through which current pioneers have already journeyed. Take time to listen to someone's story and hear the variety of experiences and expectations he or she has carried into older age.
3. Be ready to learn new ways of communicating to older people. What words do you use and how well do you listen? Are older people marginalized in your local congregation because their voices cannot be heard?
4. Understand the changing scene. The third and fourth ages bring differing experiences and fears. How are people enabled to reconcile fears of ailment, limitation and loss? Transport older people to church when they are unable to get there themselves, train people to visit housebound older members, and never be afraid of entering a nursing home!

5. Prepare people for retirement, for the changes in status, activity, and relationship, and support them through this time of great change. Do not assume that because someone retires he or she automatically becomes available for all the jobs in the church that no one else wants!

6. Do not assume because someone is older he or she is holy! Do not be afraid to challenge where necessary those who are growing older. Are they growing older in Christ? Do they seek in their own lives to live a full age displaying Jesus to those around them?

7. Provide a voice for older witnesses of Christ and uphold them within the church. Give opportunity for testimony, either spoken or written. Use these voices in mission perhaps by collating stories of faith to be distributed in your area.

8. Enable those who have lived long in the faith to encourage those who are new. Establish mentoring schemes between young and old. But let these be a two-way learning process. Such schemes can also be used in outreach to local schools and organizations.

9. Learn from people already doing this! Read books like; Albert Jewell (ed.), *Older People and the Church* (Methodist Publishing House, 2001); Albert Jewell (ed.), *Ageing and Spirituality* (Jessica Kingsley, 1999); Michael Apichella, *The Church's Hidden Asset: Empowering the Older Generation* (Kevin Mayhew, 2001); Ian Knox, *Older People and the Church* (T. & T. Clark, 2002) and Rhena Taylor's *Three Score Years – and Then?* (Monarch, 2001). All are currently in print.

10. Finally, preach the gospel in season and out of season to men and women of all ages. Never exclude the older person from hearing the gospel of Jesus Christ from lack of awareness, preparation or desire. For Christ died for all.

Bibliography

Print-based sources

Adamson, J., *The Epistle of James* (Eerdmans, 1976)

Allen, L.C., *The Books of Joel, Obadiah, Jonah and Micah* (Eerdmans, 1976)

Apichella, M., *The Church's Hidden Asset: Empowering the Older Generation* (Kevin Mayhew, 2001)

Atkinson, D. *The Message of Job* (Inter-Varsity Press, 1991)

——, *The Message of Ruth* (Inter-Varsity Press, 1983)

Bauman, Z., *The Individualized Society* (Polity, 2001)

Baur, C., *John Chrysostom and his Time* Vol. 1 (Sands, 1959)

Beagon, P., *Social and Political Aspects of the Career of St Basil of Caesarea* (Unpublished DPhil Thesis, Oxford University, 1990)

Best, R., 'The Spiritual Role of the Elder in the Twenty-first Century' in D.O. Moberg (ed.), *Aging and Spirituality* (Haworth Pastoral Press, 2001)

Bianchi, E.C., 'A Spirituality of Aging' in L.S. Cahill and D. Mieth (eds), 'Aging', special edition of *Concilium* Vol. 3 (SCM Press, 1991)

Biggs, S., *The Mature Imagination: Dynamics of Identity in Midlife and Beyond* (Open University Press, 1999)

——, *Understanding Ageing: Images, Attitudes and Professional Practice* (Open University Press, 1993)

Blaikie, A., *Ageing and Popular Culture* (Cambridge University Press, 1999)

Bond, J., Coleman P. and Peace, S. (eds), *Ageing in Society* (Sage, 1993^2).

Boyle, C., 'Love in an Older Climate', *The Guardian*, 20 July 2000.

Bright, R., *Wholeness in Later Life* (Jessica Kingsley, 1997)

Brodie, I., 'America's Elderly fill Sunset Days with Crime', *The Times*, 24 October 2000

Brown, C.G., *The Death of Christian Britain* (Routledge, 2001)

Brueggemann, W., *Genesis* (John Knox Press, 1982)

——, *The Message of the Psalms: A Theological Commentary* (Augsburg, 1984)

Campbell, R.A., *The Elders: Seniority in Earliest Christianity* (T. & T. Clark, 1994)

Carson, D., *The Gospel According to John* (IVP, 1994)

Church of England Board of Social Responsibility, *Ageing* (Church House, 1990)

Clarke, W.K.L., *The Ascetic Works of St Basil* (SPCK, 1925)

Coleman, P., 'Adjustment in Later Life' in J. Bond, P. Coleman and S. Peace (eds), *Ageing in Society* (Sage, 1993^2)

Common Worship (Church House, 2000)

Constantelos, D.J., *Byzantine Philanthropy and Social Welfare* (Rutgers University Press, 1968)

Davids, P.H., *The First Epistle of Peter* (Eerdmans, 1990)

Davie, G., *Religion in Britain Since 1945* (Blackwell, 1994)

Davies, J.G., *Daily Life in the Early Church* (Lutterworth, 1952)

Department of Social Security Inter-Ministerial Group for Older People, *Life Begins at 50: A Better Society for Older People*, May 2000

Drane, J., *Cultural Change and Biblical Faith* (Paternoster, 2001)

Encomium of Saint Gregory, Bishop of Nyssa, on his Brother Saint Basil, Archbishop of Cappadocian Caesarea, Sister J.A. Stein (tr.) (The Catholic University of America, 1928)

Evangelical Alliance, 'The Role of Christian Churches and Groups in Society', conducted by MORI Social Research in March 2002

Faulkner, T.M. and De Luce, J., *Old Age in Greek and Latin Literature* (State of New York University Press, 1989)

Finley, M.I., 'The Elderly in Classical Antiquity' in T.M. Faulkner and J. De Luce, *Old Age in Greek and Latin Literature* (State of New York University Press, 1989)

Ford, R., 'Identity Thieves are a Threat to your Future', *The Times*, 25 March 2000

France, R.T., *Matthew* (IVP, 1985)

Gibson, H.B. *Loneliness in Later Life* (Macmillan, 2000)

Ginn, J., 'Grey Power: Age-based Organisations' Response to Structured Inequalities', *Critical Social Policy* 38, Autumn 1993

Green, J.B., *The Gospel of Luke* (Eerdmans, 1997)

Green, P., *Old Age and the Life to Come* (A.A. Mowbray, 1950)

Guenther, M., *Toward Holy Ground: Spiritual Directions for the Second Half of Life* (Darton, Longman & Todd, 1996)

Hall, S., 'Half Over 80s Exist on £80 a Week or Less', *The Guardian*, 5 October 1999

Harris, J.G., *God and the Elderly* (Fortress Press, 1987)

Hartley, J.E., *The Book of Job* (Eerdmans, 1988)

Hastings, A., *A History of English Christianity 1920–2000* (SCM, 2001)

Howarth, C., Kenway, P., Palmer, G. and Street, C., *Monitoring Poverty and Social Exclusion: Labour's Inheritance* (Joseph Rowntree Foundation, York)

Howse, K., *Religion, Spirituality and Older People* (Centre for Policy on Ageing, 1999)

Hughes, G.W., 'Is There a Spirituality for the Elderly? An Ignation Approach' in A. Jewell (ed.), *Spirituality and Ageing* (Jessica Kinsgley, 1999)

'Internet Access June 2001' issued by National Statistics Office, London

Jamieson, A., *A Churchless Faith: Faith Journeys Beyond the Churches* (SPCK, 2002)

Jardine, C., 'Woopie', first published in *The Telegraph* in November 1994, quoted in C. Donnellan (ed.), *Our Ageing Generation* Vol. 16 (Independence, 1995)

Jenkins, S., 'Old Enough to Know Better', *Third Way*, March 1999

Jerrome, D., 'Intimate Relationships' in J. Bond, P. Coleman and S. Peace (eds), *Ageing in Society* (Sage, 1993²)

Jewell, A. (ed.), *Older People and the Church* (Methodist Publishing House, 2001)

——, *Spirituality and Ageing* (Jessica Kingsley, 1999)

Johnson, M., 'Dependency and Interdependency' in J. Bond, P. Coleman and S. Peace (eds), *Ageing in Society* (Sage, 1993²)

Johnson, P. and Thane, P. (eds), *Old Age from Antiquity to Postmodernity* (Routledge, 1998)

Kelly, J.N.D., *Golden Mouth: The Story of John Chrysostom – Ascetic, Preacher, Bishop* (Gerald Duckworth, 1995)

Kertzer, D.I. and Laslett, P., *Aging in the Past: Demography, Society and Old Age* (University of California Press, 1995)

Kidner, D., *Psalms 1–72* (Inter-Varsity Press, 1973)

Kirkwood, T., *The End of Age: Why Everything about Ageing is Changing* (Profile, 2001)

Koenig, H., McCullough, M.E. and Larson, D.B., *Handbook of Religion and Health* (Oxford University Press, 2001)

Kraus, H.J., *Psalms 60 – 150: A Continental Commentary*, Hilton C. Oswald (tr.) (Augsburg Fortress, 1989)

Landale, J., Peek, L. and Jacob, G., 'Blair Urged to Buy Back the Pensioner Vote', *The Times*, 15 May 2000

Lomax Cook, F. and Settersten, R.A., 'Expenditure Patterns by Age and Income among Mature Adults: Does Age Matter?', *The Gerontologist* Vol. 35 No. 1 (The Gerontological Society of America, 1995)

MacKinlay, E., *The Spiritual Dimension of Ageing* (Jessica Kingsley, 2001)

Maffesoli, M. *The Time of the Tribes: The Decline of Individualism in Mass Society*, Don Smith (tr.) (Sage, 1996)

Marshall, I.H., *The Gospel of Luke* (Paternoster Press, 1998)

Martin, D., *A General Theory of Secularisation* (Blackwell, 1978)

Martin, R.P., *James* (Word, 1988)

McGrath, A.E., *Christian Spirituality* (Blackwell, 1999)

——, *The Journey: A Pilgrim in the Lands of the Spirit* (Hodder & Stoughton, 1999)

Meggitt, J.J., *Paul, Poverty and Survival* (T. & T. Clark, 1998)

Merchant, R., 'Cell Church: Culturally Appropriate?' in M. Green (ed.), *Church Without Walls: A Global Examination of Cell Church* (Paternoster, 2002)

Metropolitan Anthony of Sourozh, 'The Spirituality of Old Age' in A. Jewell, *Spirituality and Ageing* (Jessica Kingsley, 1999)

Moberg, D.O. (ed.), *Aging and Spirituality* (Haworth Pastoral Press, 2001)

Motyer, A., *Isaiah* (Inter-Varsity Press, 1999)

Mounce, W.D., *Pastoral Epistles* (Word, 2000)

Moynagh, M., *Changing World, Changing Church* (Monarch, 2001)

Murphy, R.E., *Ecclesiastes* (Word, 1992)

——, *Proverbs* (Thomas Nelson, 1988)

Nicholson-Lord, D., 'Mass Leisure Class is on the Way, say Forecasters', *The Independent*, April 1994

Niebuhr, H.R., *Christ and Culture* (Faber & Faber, 1952)

Nolland, J., *Luke 1 – 9:20* (Word, 1989)

Oswalt, J.N., *The Book of Isaiah: Chapters 40 – 66* (Eerdmans, 1998)

Parkin, T., 'Ageing in Antiquity: Status and Participation' in P. Johnson and P. Thane (eds), *Old Age from Antiquity to Postmodernity* (Routledge, 1998)

Pensioners' Incomes Series 1999/00 (Office of National Statistics, 2000)

Phillipson, C., Bernard, M., Phillips, M. and Ogg, J., *The Family and Community Life of Older People* (Routledge, 2001)

Prior, D., *The Message of Joel, Micah and Habakkuk* (Inter-Varsity Press, 1998)

Radda, K.E., Schensul, J.J., Burkholder, G.J., Ward, E. and Levy, J., 'Intimate Contacts: Older Adults at Risk, Sexual Activities and HIV Risk' in programme abstracts from the 54th Annual Meeting of the Gerontological Society of America, *The Gerontologist* Vol. 41 Special Issue 1, October 2001 (The Gerontological Society of America, 2001)

Richards, K., 'The Adventure of Living', *Contact*, May 1969

Roscoe, L.A., Malphurs, J.E., Dragovic, L.J. and Cohen, D., 'A Comparison of Characteristics of Kevorkian Euthanasia Cases and Physician Assisted Suicides in Oregon', *The Gerontologist* Vol. 41 No. 4 (The Gerontological Society of America, 2001)

Rousseau, P., *Basil of Caesarea* (University of California Press, 1994)

Saunders, J., *Dementia: Pastoral Theology and Pastoral Care* (Grove, 2002)

Scheper, T. and Duursma, S., 'Euthanisa: The Dutch Experience' in *Age and Ageing* (Oxford University Press, 1994)

Scrutton, S., *Counselling Older People* (Arnold, 1999²)

Senior A. and Stewart, C., 'Promises with a Silver Lining', *The Times*, 19 May 2001

Sparks, A., '*Church Family? Intergenerational Tension in the Church*' (unpublished essay)

Stead, F.H., *The Story of Social Christianity* Vol. 1 (James Clarke, 1924)

Stuttaford, T., 'STDs – Sex and the Sixties', *The Times*, 10 July 2001

Summerskill, B., 'Elderly Lose Faith in Religion', *The Guardian*, 3 September 2000

Tate, M.E., *Psalms 51–100* (Word, 1990)

Taylor, R., *Three Score Years – and Then?* (Monarch, 2001)

Tkach, V,. 'Tomorrow's World', *Investors Chronicle* Vol. 137/1745 (Financial Times Business 17–23 August 2001)

Trends in Life Expectancy by Social Class 1972–1999 (Office of National Statistics, 2002)

Tromans, E., 'Older Models … Faces of the Present', *Saga Magazine*, April 2002

VanGemeren, W.A. (ed.), *New International Dictionary of Old Testament Theology and Exegesis* (Paternoster, 1997)

Varela, J.I.G., 'The Costa Rican Experience: Protestant Growth and Desertion in Costa Rica: Viewed in Relation to Churches with Higher Attrition Rates, Lower Attrition Rates, and More Mobility' in H. Wraight (ed.), *They Call Themselves Christian* (Christian Research, 1999)

Walter, T., *The Revival of Death* (Routledge, 1997)

Webber, A., *Life Later On: Older People and the Church* (Triangle, 1990)

Web-based sources

An online text of the Didache can be viewed at < www. newadvent.org/fathers/0714.htm >.

Nicene and Post-Nicene Fathers texts are available online at < www.ccel.org/fathers2/ >.

The web address for Action on Elder Abuse is < www. elderabuse.org >. If you would like further help or assistance contact AEA at Action on Elder Abuse, Astral House, 1268 London Road, London SW16 4ER, UK. Telephone: 0208 764 7648; e-mail: < aea@ace.org.uk >.

W.D. Novelli, 'The Social Dimension of Sustainable Development' at < www.aarp.org/intl/speech.html > (accessed 14 May 2002).

For *Saga Magazine* details see < www.saga.co.uk >.

J.P. Fowler, 'Why Me? The Truth about HIV' at < www. arrp.org/mmaturity/jul_aug00/whyme.html >. First published 2000.

Government Expenditure Plans 2000–2001: these figures from the Department of Health can be viewed at < www.doh.gov.uk/dohreport/report2000/dr2000–03.html >.

The Age Concern Fact Sheet is available online at < www. ageconcern.org.uk >.

The United Nations website can be viewed at < www. un.org > This site has an excellent archive facility. See also < www.un.org/ageing > for details about the World Congress on Ageing held in Madrid 2002. The document 'Implications of an Ageing Society' can be viewed at < www.un.org/esa/socdev/ageing/ageimpl.htm > (accessed 19 May 2002). To read Kofi Annan's statement accompanying the launch of the 1999 International Year of Older Persons see < www.un.org/esa/socdev/iyop/iyopsgsm.htm > (accessed 14 May 2002).

No Secrets: The Protection of Vulnerable Adults (The Department of Health, March 2000). See p. 7 for definition of vulnerable adults. Copies of the report can be viewed at < www.doh.gov.uk/scg/nosecrets.htm >.

C. Reeve, 'Spirituality in the Third Age' can be viewed at < www.thirdage.com/features/healthy/spiritual/index.html > (accessed 14 May 2002).

The AARP 2000 Annual Report, 'Your Choice, Your Voice, Your Attitude', is available in pdf format from < www.aarp.org/ar/2000 >.

T. Macnair, *Elderly People and Depression*, BBC Online, 26 October 2000 can be viewed at < www.bbc.co.uk/health/features/depression_elderly.shtml > (accessed 2 October 2001).

Go to < www.bbc.co.uk/radio4/reith2001/ > for texts of the Reith Lectures.

Recordings of all conference lectures from the second International Conference on Ageing, Spirituality and Wellbeing, held in Durham, UK, in July 2002, can be obtained through the conference convenors, The MHA Care Group, or the Christian Council on Ageing. A book of conference lectures and workshops will be available in 2003.